The Mother You Know

By

Evelyn Wooten McGovern

Co-authored by Phenomenal Women

2022

unconditional love   I love my mother

she did the best she could   young mother

The Mother You Know

mom worked very hard   she did love me

I love my mother   al love

young mother   could

family secret   orgiveness

my mother had   dora's box

she did lo   non   d very hard

uncondit   e my mother

she did the best   young mother

by Evelyn Wooten McGovern

First Printing: 2022

ISBN: 979-8-9860894-6-1

Ordering Information:

Special discounts are available on quantity purchases by corporations, associations, educators, and others. For details, contact the publisher at the email listed below.

U.S. trade bookstores and wholesalers:
Please contact info@businessofbooksmastermind.com.

DEDICATION

I dedicate this book in honor of my mother, Dorothy Wooten (the mother I know!), my husband Patrick McGovern for always supporting me, my twin sons Jawain and Cawain, Women of Colors, and future generations of my family.

As for my legacy, **it is what it is!**

A MESSAGE FOR MOTHERS

Thank you for loving your sons and daughters unconditionally, teaching them about their place and purpose in the world, and modeling the values of faith and forgiveness.

Thank you for instilling joy and gratitude for life in your children.

Thank you for serving as an example of service by practicing volunteerism in and beyond your community.

Thank you for inspiring your children to use their gifts and talents to build a better world.

Thank you for pushing your sons and daughters outside their comfort zones to help them grow into the best versions of themselves.

Thank you for treating the people you encounter with respect, dignity, and love so that your sons and daughters may touch lives in the same way.

Thank you for teaching your children—directly or indirectly—about selflessness and sacrifice.

Thank you for lending a helping hand, a listening ear, or a compassionate heart when you meet someone who needs your gifts.

Thank you for changing the world in loud and quiet ways.

Thank you for armoring your children in courage, compassion, and conviction.

Thank you for strengthening your children with love.

Thank you for helping others without agenda or judgment.

Thank you for being your kids' lifelong cheerleaders, for believing in them, and most importantly, for teaching them to believe in themselves.

Thank you for blessing your children with the world and for blessing the world with your children.

~Poem Submitted Anonymously

TABLE OF CONTENTS

INTRODUCTION

The central message of *The Mother You Know* is that sometimes we think we know our parents or our mother, but in essence, many times, we really don't. We don't know our mother's stories, so this is the opportunity to see or read different women's stories about their mothers and what they know of their mothers.

The idea for a book about motherhood came about at a membership meeting for Women of Colors (WOC). I am the president of WOC, a nonprofit organization serving communities in and around Saginaw, Michigan. The meeting was called "The Mother You Know," it was an opportunity for each of us to honor our mothers and talk about our mothers and our experiences. There were about ten women at this meeting, and of the ten women, it seemed like almost everyone had a compelling story to tell about her mother; there wasn't a dry eye in the room.

There was only one member who really had nothing to share. She couldn't find or didn't know anything about her mother that questioned her motherhood. But all the women had a lot of things going on in their mothers' lives that affected them to the day of our meeting. Years and years—even decades—later, the experiences of growing up under the nurturance of their mother had affected them in some form or fashion, whether good or bad.

For context, Women of Colors meetings often have themes—for example, "The Mother You Know." We use themes more so now than before. We try to have programs that are educational and empowering because we're all about empowering women. For many membership meetings, we'll have speakers. The talk might be about leadership, or it might be about what you can do to serve in the community in terms of volunteerism. There are a lot of components to Women of Colors. That's why we include the "s" on "Colors"—because we do so many things with so many different people.

I chose to create this book as a story collection with multiple authors contributing because I felt readers would benefit from this style and format of book. I thought *The Mother You Know* would be a unique book, especially from five African American women talking about our upbringing because that's just something you don't usually read or hear about in conversation. So, it's a form of enrichment. Our story is one that many have, but no one shares. It's like Pandora's box. How do we grow—how do we begin to expand—if we don't tell these stories and try not to repeat the errors of our ways or problems that occurred in the past? Writing this book provided a way of healing for me.

In this book, we let other mothers know that they're not alone—their struggles are ours alike. And there's no perfect mother. There's no perfect human being on this earth, so how could there be a perfect mother? We make mistakes. All mothers make mistakes. Some are greater than others, but no matter what mistake a mother makes, she is still their mother if she births a child. She affects them in some form or fashion. No matter what your mother has done, it's not like you can't overcome your animosity for her. Sometimes mothers can't help the traumas that have happened to them that may have prevented them from being present in your life physically or emotionally.

The Mother You Know is a collection of different stories from women who have overcome so many barriers to love their mothers. And they're doing well despite all the disparities that have happened in their life. In addition to telling my story in chapter one, I invited four women to contribute stories to this book. First, Sandra Wooten is my younger sister. Second, Marcia Reeves is a good friend whom I met at church. Third, Lula Woodard is a member of WOC who has held several office positions over twenty-plus years. Finally, Vicki Hill is the vice-chair for WOC and a good friend.

This book leaves a legacy for these women and their families because it retells their stories. It leaves a legacy for their generation. I know hardly anything about my grandparents—my parents didn't tell me any stories to really teach me or tell me about their parents—and that bothers me. So, this book is especially for Sandra's, Marcia's, Lula's, and Vicki's kids and their kids' kids. We should be telling our stories to teach our kids what can happen and what has and shouldn't happen. That's why I'm passionate about this project.

In gathering these individual stories and designing the interviews, several questions were influential in shaping each contributor's chapter and the book as a whole. One interview question that stands out in my mind is, "What was your view on your mother as a child versus as an adult?" There's usually a transition from being a child to becoming a woman or man regarding views about your mother. You learn things. You notice more prevalent things, whether your mother was more nurturing or wasn't as nurturing compared to other mothers.

For many people, it is not evident during childhood that something is missing. Getting older can unearth things about our mothers that went unnoticed or unacknowledged as children. Someone might realize as an adult, "Hey, my mom never hugged me like that." They don't really have a point of reference to compare their experiences to until they enter adulthood. To me, this is very powerful because people change as they get older; things they used to believe, they don't anymore.

The five stories within this book share a lot of common ground. In most stories, the moms had to learn how to be strong and persevere. Another thread connecting our stories is love: love from a mother, love for a mother, or both. No matter what these women went through with their mothers, they felt love from their mothers, even though they were all shown affection in different ways. And that's just amazing!

Co-authoring this book taught me that you don't have control of other people's lives. You can't force anyone to do anything, only yourself to be a better person. You have to love your mother unconditionally, just like your mother should love you—it is always possible to love another human being unconditionally, especially your mother.

I feel the need to emphasize: There are a lot of individuals struggling with their mothers. They're not going to come out and tell you—but many people are living in anguish and pain. When these folks read these stories and experience the transparency, they may realize that others have been through worse than they have and still love their mother.

The Mother You Know is nonfiction. These are real-life stories that we lived. We made it to the other side and figured out, at the end of the day, it's still about love.

All five of our stories reflect on love and motherhood, but each story is unique. We went through our struggles at different ages. We were in different places in life geographically and socioeconomically. In my story, as in the other women's stories, I reflect on the journey of discovering my mother as a woman and human being than what I knew in my childhood.

Of course, some people don't really care or don't want to know their mothers' history or never thought about it—there are all kinds of scenarios. But most of us want to know the history of our mothers. More than any other human being on this earth, we should want to know about our mothers.

The intended meaning behind the title *The Mother You Know* is to ask the questions: Do you think you know your mother? Do you know your mother's story? Do you know her history? Your mother's history may be different from her story. These three questions are powerful because most people don't know these answers. Further, how do you find peace when you don't know your mother's story and history, both the good and the bad?

I want the world to be able to explore different views on how people have lived their lives, how they've been birthed into this world, and how they've transitioned into adulthood to become productive adults despite their struggles. I want to put this book out into the universe to help individuals who are really, truly struggling with their mothers in hopes that they will find some solace in the fact that they're not alone. I want to show other human beings that it's possible to overcome anything if they've lost a mother, their mother abandoned them, or whatever the case may be. There's still hope—and there's still love—in this world.

This collection can serve as a healing book for readers. I know there are a lot of readers who are hurting because of how their mother may have raised them. There might have been some outside forces that affected their mother's way of raising her children or her child. I want readers to be able to forgive, and no matter what, I hope that they love their mother because she brought them into this world.

Daughters and sons are often struggling with something that deals with their mother. They have to be able to heal; for them to heal, they have to forgive.

First and foremost, they have to forgive their mother no matter what she has done. It could have been that she had a mental illness. And if people with mental illnesses don't get treatment, what happens? Their loved ones get hurt.

Another thing to consider is maybe your mom's mother or father had some mental illness problems going on, and who knows how it could have affected your mom. That's why people should research and understand their family's history.

There's always a powerful story around any life. Thank God people are starting to tell their stories and express themselves in authentic ways. To me, watching TV involves nothing of substance. You see a lot of reality TV shows now, but what is a "reality show?" Does it talk about real life, how people really act and talk? Of course not. This isn't a game. These are real people's lives. I hope this book heals relationships, especially mother-daughter and mother-son relationships.

If there is one key takeaway I expect or hope to impart to the daughters, mothers, and grandmothers who read *The Mother You Know*, it's that they love their bloodline, their motherhood line, and their relationship with their mother to eternity. As far as I'm concerned, there's nothing greater than the love that you have for a mother and nothing stronger than a mother's love.

LIST OF AUTHORS IN CHAPTER ORDER

1. Evelyn Wooten McGovern
2. Sandra Wooten
3. Marcia Reeves
4. Lula R. Woodard
5. Vicki Hill

THE MOTHER EVELYN KNOWS
Evelyn Wooten McGovern

My mother, Dorothy Mae Ledbetter, was employed with General Motors (GM) for over fifteen years. She loved going to church, and because she had a beautiful voice, she used to sing in the church choir and for multiple gospel groups, often performing solo. Other churches even requested my mother to sing solo; some of the people in the congregations would scream, "Hallelujah," and dance until they ended down on the floor. Mom loved to dress up for church; in fact, she had so many church clothes, dress shoes, and hats to match that she used an entire bedroom as a closet in her home. Perhaps this is why my siblings and I like to dress up to this day! I remember my mother as a friendly and caring person with a giving heart. Her family and friends, especially her children, gravitated toward her.

I was close to my mother, but you tend to take this closeness for granted as a child. You worship the ground your mother walks on. I grew up in a household of six people—my father, mother, three siblings, and me. I thought we had the perfect family. We went to church every Sunday. My father was an usher, and my mother sang in the choir every Sunday at Tabernacle Baptist Church. She liked for us, her children, to carry ourselves respectfully, and she never disrespected us in any way. Our mother gave us values where we respected ourselves and other people. She taught us to treat people the way we wanted to be treated. In addition, she was always giving and the life of the party. Whenever there was a special holiday, she gave lots of gifts, and we always enjoyed being around her.

My dad used to be a sharecropper in Arkansas, and he later moved to Saginaw, Michigan, and worked for GM. He built our family a beautiful home from the ground up, and although he was not the type to play with his children, he was all about providing for his family. My dad worked every day; sometimes, he held two or three jobs just to make ends meet.

:::::

One day I came home, and my mom was not there. I did not know why. From that moment on, my family's life really changed. Within months, my mom and dad decided to get a divorce. My older brother was old enough to live independently, but we younger children had to go to court and tell the judge which parent we wanted to live with, which was hard. But finally, I decided I wanted to live with my mother. My twin brother made the same decision. My baby sister chose to live with our dad.

Later, my mom decided to marry someone else. But the man she married was flawed, and his character was the total opposite of my dad's. With my dad, we never heard him curse. He always went to church. We never saw him drink. As a matter of fact, we never heard our parents argue. However, my mother's second husband drank, used a lot of foul language, and was just awful. I wondered how she went from marrying my father to marrying a man who did not treat her like a queen.

My stepfather was supposed to be a preacher! He was very intimidating and controlling—and always liked to carry. My stepdad even carried his weapon in the church pulpit. He personified and embodied the image of the famous motion-picture actor John Wayne the cowboy. He tried to dress, walk, and act like John Wayne. Seriously, he wore a western gun belt and holster that fit a 45-Long Colt. I disliked my stepfather for the pain he caused my entire family, and I felt I would never forgive him for his discretions.

My mother was a victim of domestic violence. I remember one time I was challenging my mom to help get her to leave my stepdad because he was the most unpleasant man I had ever met. He abused my mother mentally, emotionally, verbally, and physically. I saw and heard this all the time. He made idle threats, but he never touched my brother or me. One day, I finally said, "If you really love me like you say you do, Mom, please leave him. Why don't you leave him? Why would you stay?"

Mom tried many times to leave my stepdad and returned. Once, we moved all the way to Sacramento, California, to live with my mom's sister to get away from him. My mother even enrolled my brother and me in an elementary school. I thought this was our new fresh start traveling over two thousand miles to get away from my stepdad. However, I noticed my mom seemed more distressed during this time, which caused us to immediately return to Michigan three months later to return to my stepdad. I could not understand why my mom chose to go back. I did not want to leave her with this mad man! I thought I was my mother's keeper, and I needed to protect her from all harm and danger.

I can often remember us walking down the sidewalks of Bay City, Michigan, each of us (my mom, my twin brother, and myself) with our suitcases in tow in the middle of winter, not knowing where we were going to stay that night. We would be gone for two or three days, sometimes not that long, which was humiliating and embarrassing. Ultimately, we would end up right back where we left, right back at the house with my dreadful stepdad; this posed a difficult childhood for my siblings and me.

The first challenge I faced was not being home with my biological dad. It devastated the entire dynamics of our family unit. My mom's relationship with our stepdad divided us even more as a family. I had to watch my mother stay in an abusive relationship constantly. On one occasion, I remember getting a round, black, cast-iron skillet, and I was about to hit that man over the head with it when he had both of his hands around my mother's neck. I could hear my mother gasping for air. After he noticed me with the cast-iron skillet, he immediately stopped choking my mother. At this moment, I knew I posed a threat to him, and if I stayed, matters would only get worse. He wanted to put me out of his house after this incident. I was proud of myself for having the courage to defend my mother, but I could not make my mom leave him no matter what.

My stepdad also acted like a drunken fool! He was ordinarily mild, meek, and quiet; however, when he drank, he became crazy. For several years, my siblings and I had been putting up with unhealthy relationships. I did not let my stepdad off the hook by not holding him accountable for what he had done to my mother. But what could I do that would not be illegal or detrimental to my well-being?

On one particular day, I was twelve years old, and my stepdad called me an obscene name, "bitch." And at that moment, I said to myself, "You know what? I must go! I can't stay any longer." I told my mom I loved her, but I could not do it anymore. My mother could not love herself during this time, so how could I expect her to love me?

After so many instances of being disrespected, I just could not take any more disrespect, and I had to make the decision for myself. I had no control over my mom and stepdad's relationship. I had to consider what I needed to do and what would be best for me. I decided to move back home with my dad, Elbert L. "Sugar Pie" Wooten. My siblings and I had another home where we could stay. A lot of people do not have a second home to go to; they must endure any hardship that comes their way. I knew that my dad had a home for all his children, that he would take care of us, and wanted us all to be together. He welcomed us home with open arms. After we left my mom, a huge barrier was built between my mom and me for a long time. I knew she loved me, but I could not understand why she could not be with us. I was traumatized; I did not speak to my mom for two years after moving back with my dad. Believe it or not, my dad loved my mom until the day he died in 2019, and he never remarried.

Our dad worked the second shift, which allowed us to have a lot of unsupervised time to do whatever we wanted. He did not know half the things we used to do as kids because he worked a lot of overtime and sometimes held two jobs. We knew what time his truck would roll up in the driveway at night, and we made sure to be in bed by then. Dad favored my sister, Sandra, more because she stayed; she was the child that never left him. He was closer to her, and they had a special bond; they kept their bond when my twin and I returned to live with them. We had to recognize and accept their special relationship until the day my dad passed away four decades later.

I feel like I had a short childhood, and I had to grow up faster than my actual age at twelve years old to help my dad. Growing up, I became mentally headstrong because our childhood was tough. I washed our clothes, cleaned, and cooked the best I knew how. Privately I took on the protector role for my siblings. Without adult supervision, especially in our adolescent years, my siblings and I used to physically fight all the time. My sister, Sandra, did not want me to tell her what to do. I thought I was helping and protecting my one and only younger sister.

::::::

After graduating from Delta College, I joined the military and was part of the Army Reserves, and I moved and served my duty in Atlanta, Georgia. Later, I became pregnant out of wedlock with fraternal twin boys who looked nothing alike. After my sons, Jawain and Cawain, were born, I asked my mom to come and stay with us for two weeks so she could help with them; she agreed to come.

My mom was a different type of person during this visit. She was on edge a lot, did not seem well, and was not her usual, cheerful self. I watched her constantly because I was worried about her. One night, she was in the guest bedroom, and I thought she was talking to someone. I went and peeked in the room. My mother was sitting on the floor in a fetal position, talking to herself like she was hearing voices. That night, I picked up a negative vibration and prayed to God to please intercede: "Please, God, help my mother and let her be all right." When I woke up the next morning, I immediately called my Aunt Lorean to share with her what was happening to my mom, as I was fearful something was seriously wrong with her. I described my mother as being highly distressed. "It's like she's possessed or something," I said. "What's going on?" My aunt recommended we get her back home right away.

My aunt and I believed that someone had used witchcraft against my mom. Thus, we needed to find a way to release her from the bad spirits. At this point, I recalled a memorable childhood experience with a "magic man" who practiced spiritual healing out of his basement in Pontiac, Michigan.

When I was a child, about nine years old, the adults around me would play the numbers to win cash like the lottery. Many people traveled to Pontiac to receive lucky numbers. One time I went along with my mom and auntie to get their lucky numbers, and I had a chance to see this magic man. I remember going into his basement because that is where he operated. As we went into the dark basement, I saw the magic man sitting in a small hut covered with lots of essential items, including a crystal ball. He was spooky looking with long, black, matted hair. I could not see his eyes with dark glasses covering his face. The hut looked like a shrine of mysterious items and smelled like a strong, fragrant smoke from burning incense.

Speaking with my aunt, I determined I wanted this magic man to heal my mother. Neither my mom nor my aunt practiced voodooism or anything like that. But they did trust this man because they heard so much good about what he did through his practice for other people. People waited hours to see this magic man, popular among customers who needed spiritual healing or wanted lucky numbers. I know this is unexplainable and mysterious, but this happened. The human faculty can be used for good and bad reasons. People do not talk about voodooism; they keep it a family secret in Pandora's box.

Here is the letter my mother wrote about "The Magic Man," in her own words after seeing the Magic Man.

I don't keep a headache all the time now. He told me to take Sineoff and they did the job. He said if I had given up and didn't have a strong belief in God, I would have been dead and all the trouble and disgrace we had was because somebody didn't want us to do good. They wanted me to be a failure and disgrace, but the Lord works in mysterious ways. I didn't know you was that concerned about me in fact because of what happened and some of the things I did you was ashamed to be around me. I was kind of leery about coming to visit you. He also told me to take the Aleve for my bleeding, but I haven't taken any of that yet since the doctor said I have to take these pills for the rest of my time or until God see fit for me to stop. This is to avoid an operation, but I am going to ask the Magic Man.

I heard from my aunt about what happened when she took my mother to see this man. He said that somebody had practiced voodooism against my mom, and she was sick. At this point, my mother was having trouble with her mind, and she was going downhill fast. My mother told me that the man performed ritual magic to summon up spirits to command them to set her free. Afterward, the magic man instructed my mom on what to do and gave her a list of steps she should follow when she returned home. I know my aunt had to pay quite a bit of money for this service. My mom did what the magic man asked her to do—and she got better, which was unbelievably wonderful. But at this point, I still questioned whether it was the magic man who helped her. Was it really the magic this healer performed or was it just by fate that my mother got better for other reasons?

What solidified it for me was the description he gave of the lady who had practiced witchcraft against my mother. The lady he described was a close friend of hers. Now, my mother and my aunt told me that they had not reversed anything or tried to practice voodooism against this woman. Still, on that same day, my mom visited the magic man to release the bad spirits thrust upon her, my mother's friend immediately became sick and went to the hospital.

:::::

When I attended Delta College, I remember writing a report about voodooism. My research revealed that whether we realize it or not, we all could have the ability to perform psychic or faith healing. For example, parents often do this to help their children. Voodooism is defined by Oxford Languages as "a religious practice in parts of the Caribbean and the southern United States, combining elements of Roman Catholic rituals with traditional African magical and religious rites and characterized by sultry and a spirit possession."

Imagine being an innocent child and then finding out your mother's been possessed by evil spirits from a best friend all those years later. I realized that the cards were against my mom for a long time and that she could not love herself, let alone anyone else because she had all these evil spirits working against her.

After seeing the woman who brought me into this world lying helplessly in the fetal position, I am grateful for the magic man. In this experience, it was just so unusual for me even to have that discernment to recognize what was happening with my mother and know the issue was something other than medical. I can sometimes sense it when something is not right with a person, and I pick up a negative vibration. That night, the decision I made was indescribable; I feel I saved my mother's life. I do not like to tell this story, but it needs to be said to (hopefully) help someone. From my story, I hope this will help other families be more aware of their surroundings and who they trust in their family's circle.

As I was writing this chapter, I kept wondering, "Should I share specific parts of my story or not?" But voodooism is a huge part of what was significantly important in my story. Telling my mother's story without talking about voodooism is like building a house without putting in the plumbing. The story would not function if I left that part out. However, I do not want to sound like a voodoo woman or come off like I practice voodooism. I never have and never will.

Consider the possibility that you know someone in your personal life, be it a friend, family member, or acquaintance going through something similar. People do practice voodooism, whether you believe it or not. It is very underground. You do not know why people do some things they do. Suddenly, they lose their mind. And you wonder, "Well, why did they? How did they lose their mind?"

Therefore, especially in the African American community, we are very leery about eating people's food or wearing other people's clothes. Or, if we move into a new home, we may sprinkle red pepper or sage around the house to protect it from any evil spirits. Voodooism is a real thing. It is more popular in the southern United States; thus, people may travel south to get whatever they need to practice, bring it back north, and do what they think is fitting to change somebody or something.

I realized from this experience what was causing my mother's weaknesses. As a child, I did not know that she had depression, low self-esteem, and other problems. When you are young, you do not see what your parents are dealing with, and they do not come to you about their problems. But as an adult, I learned my mother was facing a lot of demons, and they were attacking her in different ways that I had not even imagined or realized. Sadly, that is one of the reasons I did not speak to my mother for two years: She was dealing with unfortunate circumstances outside of her control. However, once I realized why she was not the perfect mother, I forgave her.

I believe no matter what your mother has been through and no matter what decisions or mistakes she has made, she is still your mother. I recognize the sacrifices that my mother made. She always tried to make sure we had whatever we needed; if she had a nickel, then my siblings and I had it, too. My childhood was far from perfect, but I loved my mother.

I would tell other mothers to accept the fact that they are not perfect. There is no perfect mother. I believe we all make mistakes, and we must strive to do our best.

Keep in mind that at some point, children will want to know more about their mother. However, the mother may not want to tell them everything. My mom did not tell me that her friend practiced voodooism against her; it was something she did not even know. It is good to know where you come from and why things happened the way they have in your family; it could be from a whole host of scenarios. You may have no clue why your mother turned out as she did until you search for those reasons; this is because your understanding of a person is determined by what and how much you have seen from this individual's life and how you decipher and interpret these experiences.

My mother used to eat her best friend's food. They used to exchange clothes. My mom and dad divorced, and this wicked lady wanted my dad for himself. I could not understand why my dad never liked her or wanted his children around her. I was like, "Why?" But this was something I had to find out on my own. My mom did not tell me because she did not even know. I helped my mom figure out what was going on. She did not know. Sometimes you can find out things about your mother that you never knew, which change the whole trajectory of how you imagined her as a child. We do not always know what our mothers are going through.

::::::

Being a single parent of twin sons living in the big ATL, my mother and aunt were always worried about my boys, and they wanted us closer to our family in Michigan. I had no intentions of moving, and they would often visit us and get my sons, saying they "wanted to give me a break." What was I supposed to say? I could not refuse my mother or my aunt. I respected my aunt Lorean like a mother, and I loved her so much. She gave me my first vehicle and always was there for my family and me. She did not have children, but she was a foster parent for many children through the years. So, I adopted my aunt as my second mom.

One day I got sick, and my sons were sick as well. We all had bad colds. If I did not work, I did not get paid, and I started thinking about what if something happened to me and I could not pay my bills and take care of my children. I did not have any real family in Atlanta that could help me as I did in Michigan. So I decided to move back to Michigan. At that moment, I decided my dreams of living in Atlanta were not important enough for me to sacrifice my children's well-being, and I would do anything to make sure they had everything they needed. Once I had children, I could not put my needs first.

My stepdad was disabled at the time, and my mother needed my help. After moving back home, my boys and I lived with them for a while. At this point, I started re-establishing a connection with my mom. It was hard! My mom and I found it really difficult to build our relationship back up; however, I wanted to support my mother.

I stopped concentrating on getting my mom to leave my stepdad. His disability had progressed to the point where he could barely take care of himself, and he desperately needed my mom. So even if she wanted to walk away, she could not leave him in that condition because of her loving spirit.

Once I moved back to Michigan, I cherished and enjoyed every moment I had with my mother, especially after I found out what had happened to her. It seemed that the negative spirits left her body. She was getting better and better and was like a new person. And I am confident that it was not a regular physician practicing western medicine that healed my mother. Instead, I believe the magic man healed my mother. Because of the magic man, I got my mother back for a brief time before her fatal accident in 1992.

On July 5, 1992, my mother died in a fatal automobile accident. My twin brother, my twin sons, three cousins, and my mother were traveling from a family reunion in Osceola, Arkansas, in my Ford Aerostar van. My twin brother was driving, and I was in the front passenger seat. I do not remember what happened—my van flipped over and landed in the middle of the median on the expressway in Madrid, Missouri. The hatch popped open, and my mom fell out of the rear of my van, and she died instantly. Unfortunately, I never got to say goodbye to my mother, and this devastated me to no end.

I could not attend my mother's funeral. My pelvis had been fractured in five places. While I was recovering at the Elvis Presley Trauma Hospital in Memphis, Tennessee, I was just asking God, "Why didn't you take me instead of my mom?" I became so depressed after I lost my mom. I had never known such a pain in my life until that moment. For the first time in my life, I felt like I did not want to live anymore.

They flew me back home to Saginaw, Michigan, in a brand-new, pretty, white jet to St. Mary's Hospital the day of my mother's funeral. I still had it set in my mind that I might be able to make it to her funeral. But no, I could not attend because I could not walk, and my left leg was in traction, pulling my pelvis back into place. I was just in a depressed state of mind for months and months. It took me five months to learn how to walk again.

Once I was mobile, I became interested in a posted flyer sponsored by Neighborhood Renewal Services; this was an opportunity to bring women together to make a difference in our community. I had to find something to get me out of depression, which is when Women of Colors (WOC) was formed. WOC is an independent organization established to enhance diversity in the Great Lakes Bay Region by empowering women, mentoring youth, performing community service, and collaborating with other organizations. As today's president of WOC, my motto is, "Start, and the rest will come." WOC changed my life forever by helping me focus my loss, depression, anxiety, and disconnection on something engaging, motivational, and inspiring. I experienced serendipity in action!

I only had two years to rebuild my relationship with my mom before she passed. Time is short! You do not know how long you are going to have your mother on this earth, so it is important to work through whatever animosity you may be holding for what your mother did in her past; you do not know what happened that caused her to disappoint you in your life. Quite frankly, she may have done the best that she could, and maybe it wasn't enough, but that is all she had to give.

Your mother may have left you. She may have treated you differently than your siblings. She may have even given you up for adoption because she could not care for you physically or emotionally. No matter what, it is important to realize that the mother you know may not give an accurate or complete picture of the mother who is or was.

To have a mother is priceless. So, if she is living and breathing, whether you have a relationship with your mother or not, PLEASE be thankful. Whatever mistakes your mother has made, hopefully, you can forgive them. Because once she is gone, she is gone. And she will never come back. I forgave my mother before she passed, and I am so grateful that we shared those two years because I never had a chance to say goodbye to my mother, which was heart-breaking.

:::::

The first word that comes to mind when I think of motherhood is "pain." And the reason I say that is because of the pain a woman feels when she is in labor preparing to birth her child. But once the pain is released into the Universe, there's JOY. In motherhood, you endure and embrace the pain, loving unconditionally. You give your all, and you just hope and pray that you have done enough. Motherhood is life. You breathe life into a human being, and you hope to do your best to raise and nurture your child into a productive adult.

It is unbelievable the power of motherhood. A child may have never met their mother and not even know they are adopted, but they still feel that something is missing in their life. It's a sense of, "Why do I feel this way? What's going on?" Or, even if they have the best-adopted mother, most children still want to know who their biological mother is, no matter what.

Motherhood, to me, is loving unconditionally regardless of how you feel your children may love you. You do what you must to nurture and take care of your children. Sometimes your children may hurt you to your core (pain like you have never experienced before), but no matter how much they hurt you, you continue to love your children anyway, and that is the difficult part. Motherhood does not always feel good, but it is necessary for life.

I never planned to have children out of wedlock. In fact, I had been using protection when I became pregnant. I took precautions because I was not comfortable taking a chance on getting pregnant. It is best to know your children's paternal family history—one that I was unaware of at the time. After all, the father of your children can influence them directly and indirectly by potentially passing on any health challenges that can be transferred genetically, including physical and mental health issues.

I wanted to have one or maybe two children if I were ever to get married; however, I did not want to rush and have them at an early age and especially single. I would have liked to plan my parenthood and marriage, including plans for homeownership and a stable career path, before bearing children. At the time, this was not God's plan for me. When I got pregnant with my sons, I only wanted, prayed, and hoped for them to be healthy, safe, and loved. I can honestly say motherhood helped me develop into a better woman.

Because I did not have a stable childhood, I was determined to provide a stable life for myself and my children. It was important to me that my children never heard me speak negatively about their biological father; I did not want to jeopardize their potential to develop a relationship later.

I faced many challenges as a single parent. I had no teacher—I taught myself how to be a mother, and honestly, made many mistakes. If I had an opportunity to change some of my choices as a mother, I would. As mothers, we should also be able to apologize to our children because we do not always get it right. And if we cannot apologize to our children, then who?

I had to research, ask questions, observe other mothers, and, most of all, determine what was best for my sons. Even though I received a lot of advice from family and friends, nothing can teach a new mother everything about motherhood, except life lessons (on-the-job training). Immediately after a woman conceives a child, she acquires motherly instincts.

At first, I was upset at my mom for not better preparing me for motherhood. So I asked her, "Why didn't you tell me being a mother was going to be like this?" But she said, "This is something that really can't be told. You can read all the books you want, but until you have experienced motherhood for yourself, you will never know how you are going to feel."

As a new mother responsible for raising twin sons, I challenged myself not to compare them with each other. I had to let each of my boys be his own person, love my sons the same, unconditionally, and meet them both where they were as individuals. Each child has a unique personality, and some children require more attention than others. Children have their weaknesses and strengths. Mothers should adjust to whatever their children may need and help them be their best person.

When my twins were growing up, I tried my best to make sure that I treated each of them as an individual person. Twins tend to challenge each other, trying to prove one is better than the other, so the last thing they needed was for their mother to fuel more competition. I did not show favoritism between my sons, but I treated them differently according to their character and their choices. I used to dress my boys alike, and I enjoyed it while I could. However, as my sons got older, they did not like dressing alike, and I respected their decision.

Fostering a loving, transparent environment was important to me as my sons grew older. Every Sunday, my boys and my husband would have a family talk, and it was a no-judgment zone where my children could talk about anything. We had some deep conversations!

As a mother, I found myself duplicating some of the things my mom used to do. For instance, if my children did not think to send a birthday card to a family member or friend, I sent the card to them and put their names on the card. I wore nice Sunday dresses and hats to church and made sure that my shoes matched my purses. Although I did not have the gift of my mother's singing voice, I improvised by lip-syncing.

Being a mother means the world to me. It is part of who I am. It is in my DNA now. I cannot go a day without thinking about my twin sons. I am wondering, "Are they okay?" And when they are not okay, I am not okay. Even though they are now grown men, when they hurt, I hurt. No matter how hard I try not to feel a certain way, my feelings run deep because my sons are the best gift that God has given me.

:::::

My twin boys changed my life forever. Within a year of motherhood, I realized one of my sons, Cawain, was surprisingly special. And he was special in a way that I knew I would have to protect him even more than I could imagine. He had tendencies that were not of a boy. He was gay. And I knew before he could even walk that there was a possibility that he could be gay; I did not know for sure, but I knew there was a possibility because of his mannerisms. He portrayed female tendencies.

So, I watched my son as he grew, and the older he got, those predispositions never changed. By the time he was nine years old, I had sought therapy to help him figure out what was going on. He always tried to act like a boy, and talk like a boy. But deep down inside, I knew he was hurting. And I was hurting for him because he never really fit in anywhere.

By the time he was in high school, my son had started to change and act out. He kind of lost his way because he couldn't be who he really wanted to be. I always told him that I would love him no matter what and that he needed to be who he was born to be. I often hear people say that people can control whether they are gay or not, but I know that my son did not choose to be gay. He often wonders why him? And why is he not like his twin brother? I have done my best to raise my sons the same in terms of love; however, I could not raise them the same, as they were different.

For other mothers out there who may have a child born special, hang in there and love your child no matter what because you need them, and they need you. God makes no mistakes. I know my son was born just the way God wanted him to be.

:::::

From writing this book, I determined that if I can forgive my stepdad and the woman who hurt my mother, I can forgive anyone. Forgiveness and healing open the door for emotional growth, and each day, I strive to be a better me.

A little while after my mother's recovery, I saw the woman in the grocery store who the magic man said had practiced voodooism against my mom. I looked at her. Our eyes locked. Her eyes were fiery red! She almost looked like a devil in disguise. We greeted each other, and she looked nervous and speechless, which was out of character for her. My eyes glared at her with malice, but I kept my composure; you could have cut the tension with a knife.

Do you know what I did? About a year after I had moved back to Michigan, I took this woman a dozen red roses, and I told her I forgave her. We did not really talk about this horrible situation. We did not have to talk about what happened to my mother—we both knew. I knew what she had done based on that experience, and that was the end of it. I had to give her those roses for my sake, to release the anger and embrace forgiveness so that I could finally be released from all that was hindering me from being the best person I could be on this earth.

Years later, after my mother had passed away, I visited my stepdad, because one morning, while in the shower, I had a revelation, and I felt compelled to forgive my stepdad. I frantically cried out to God, "No, I did not want to forgive him!" When I went to visit him that afternoon, he looked frail and in poor health. I said to him, "I forgive you for the things you did to my mother." With tears in his eyes, he thanked me and apologized. He said, "I knew you would come to see me." Two weeks later, he passed away.

I feel God has given me the strength of forgiveness. I am grateful for my life despite the many challenges, and I am grateful for the mother I know. This is my story.

:::::

If your gift is to encourage others, do it! If you have money, share it generously. If God has given you leadership ability, take the responsibility seriously. And if you have a gift of showing kindness, do it gladly (Romans 12:8 [NLT]).

Don't just pretend that you love others. Really love them, Hate what is wrong. Stand on the side of the good (Romans 12:9).

EVELYN'S MOTHER:

Evelyn's Mother, Dorothy Mae Ledbetter

Evelyn's Mother

Evelyn, Mom, and siblings

ABOUT THE AUTHOR:

See Lead Author's Bio in About the Author section.

THE MOTHER SANDRA KNOWS
Sandra Kay Wooten

My mother was Dorothy Mae and my sister is Evelyn Wooten McGovern. I am the youngest of four children in the family.

My mom was easy-going, friendly, and pleasant to be around. People liked to be near her, especially her family, because she was inviting and engaging, and she tried to make people feel comfortable around her. She wasn't judgmental.

After my mom attended school for cosmetology at a place called All American Beauty School, my father remodeled our basement, creating a beauty salon room for her to do hair. Growing up, I idolized my mother because she dressed nicely. As a child, I used to love shopping with my mom, and until this day—I am a shopper! I always liked to hang out with her. Wherever she went, I wanted to go. One Saturday, she let me style her wig, and she wore it to church on Sunday—I was so proud!

My mom was a singer/soloist and a member of a gospel group that included seven members. She use to sing in the church choir and on the same stage that included groups back in the day like The Caravans, Minnie Morris, The Mighty Clouds of Joy, and The Five Blind Boys of Alabama. A lot of times when we traveled to Arkansas for the summer the church members at their family's church always wanted my mom to sing a solo. My mom always sang and I believe she enjoyed people requesting her to sing solos.

I was very close with my mother; I felt closer to her than my other siblings. I remember her as resourceful, understanding, and full of life.

:::::

When I grew a bit older, my parents decided to get a divorce, which changed our family dynamic as far as what happened in the household. Before long, I had to go to court to testify about which parent I wanted to live with and why. My sister and brother chose to live with our mother. Even though my dad was beginning to have financial hard times, I made a different choice. I felt empathetic toward my father, and I just wanted to stay at my own house with my daddy.

The first Easter that my mom was gone, my dad and I went to church. I asked him if I would get something new to wear for Easter. Dad said he didn't have the money, but he would be able to get me a new dress or a new pair of shoes—one or the other. So I chose to get the dress and wear the too-little shoes I had because I could take them off once I got to church.

I was the only child in my dad's household for a couple of years until my brother and sister moved back in with us. However, I felt alright not having my siblings with us. I was angry that we were not all living together and that they chose to live with my mom after their divorce.

Because my dad worked the second shift and sometimes held two jobs, it was difficult for him to provide us with adult supervision consistently; however, the neighbors helped watch us, and our family members pitched in when they could. I stayed with three different aunts for a couple of months during my elementary school years.

The people in the neighborhood were role models for me as a young girl. During that time, neighbors looked out for each other. If the neighbors caught me doing something incorrectly when my father wasn't home, they would let me know I was in the wrong—and eventually, they would let my dad know. As they say, it takes a village to raise a child. And it's true. My family, friends, and neighbors were my village.

:::::

I was twelve when I got pregnant with my first child. Because I was going to become a mother at such a young age, I looked for opportunities to prepare myself for motherhood during my pregnancy. Before I even got pregnant, I babysat for people, which helped. I was the youngest one in the neighborhood, and everybody looked out for each other. The family helped me, as did resources from school. At the time, continuation school was offered for pregnant women as part of the teenagers' curriculum. Because they had so many girls getting pregnant in high school during that time— I got pregnant right out of elementary school—they had to start a school with classes just for pregnant girls. Continuation school provided nurses, teachers, and other resources to help and guide me as a young mother.

Continuation school helped me learn about my body—basically like an anatomy class—and prepared me for what to expect when I went to the hospital and had the baby. The program prepares young women for what to do when they have their babies, what they will go through when they give birth, and other related topics. It pretty much gave me a heads-up on something I had no clue about at all!

I was enrolled in continuation school from the beginning of my pregnancy until six months after I had the baby. It allowed me to meet with peers and women going through the same thing as the whole class was pregnant women or new mothers. Our class included diverse women from different schools and walks of life; they were of different ages.

When I was going into labor, I knew that I was in labor. It felt like a really bad stomachache. At the time, I shared a bedroom with my sister, Evelyn; we were sleeping in bunk beds. I kept getting up to go to the bathroom, not really having to use it. Finally, the last time I got up, I crawled to the bathroom.

I still got up and dressed for school even though I was in labor. After Daddy dropped me off at school, I remember walking hunched over and needing to use the bathroom. I was worried about being gone from the classroom because I needed to be present for attendance. Eventually, my teachers asked me if I wanted to go home, so I told them to call my dad. I ended up going to the hospital.

I didn't feel like a mother once I gave birth; I felt more like a big sister babysitting. It didn't really sink in until I had to deal with motherhood all day, every day. For the first week or so, it was still a shocking feeling. But then, later, it got to the point where I knew the responsibility. My heart kicked in, and I became really nurturing.

Once I gave birth to my oldest son, I had to balance going to school with caring for my infant. In continuation school, the hours for each school day were a little shorter; however, the teachers were still preparing us to transition back to a regular school environment. I returned to traditional school the semester after my child was born.

:::::

I got pregnant for the second time at age fifteen and had the child when I was sixteen. (I had gotten pregnant for the first time at age twelve and had the child when I was thirteen.) This time, I felt more prepared and on deck. At first, I was concerned about the responsibility of having another child, but when he got here, I remember feeling like I could do it like it was no big deal. It just put a damper on having a babysitter and doing activities with friends. I couldn't do much hanging out as a teenager. I learned that if you care about your children, you can't go out all the times that you want to go.

When I became a mother, I prioritized my children over everything else. I didn't attend as many social engagements as I otherwise would have because I placed most of my focus on motherhood. I was, however, able to cultivate some friendships with other young mothers. Through my school program, I met other women navigating a similar set of challenges. We formed relationships, talked on the phone, and encouraged each other. Some of these women are still my friends today. I met at least one of my closest friends back then.

Not only was I sharing and receiving information within my friendship circles, but the other women and I provided moral support through the journey of pregnancy and parenthood. One young lady in my class, for example, asked me for a little advice on what to expect because I was older. Although this classmate was having twins, and I could not provide specific guidance in this area, I did my best to offer some general tips and words of encouragement.

Truthfully, being a young single mother involved a lot of struggles. It was hard to be available to my children all the time because I worked two or three jobs. When I had my third child, who is the youngest of my biological children, he received a lot of attention from my family members and friends. Some people misinterpreted this as me showing favoritism toward him. However, I treated all my children the same. I did a lot of work to make sure nobody really wanted for anything. I met their needs. Everybody had what they needed and sometimes what they wanted.

My aunt told me something long ago that has stuck with me. She said, "Your kids are going to do just what you do." Well, I was a handful for my dad growing up, and whenever one of my children gave me a difficult time, I knew that I had it coming! I made sure to have the oldest two sons watching my youngest, thinking, "If they babysit, they'll see what it's like to have children early, and they won't have any until they get older." And thank God, they didn't have any until they graduated from high school and were out of the house, on their own.

Each of my sons had his own personality, but my last biological child was a combination of the oldest and the middle.

:::::

I took for granted how much and how often my mother worried about me. When I had children of my own, it became my top priority to make sure they were safe at night, and that I had a safe place for them. My definition of motherhood is being a nurturer and protector.

It's better to talk to your children and build a relationship with them where they feel comfortable talking to you about anything and everything. As a mother, you can listen without being judgmental, pointing a finger, or pushing your views on them. However, remain a parent to your children, not their buddy or friend; that may come later, but be a parent first and foremost.

As someone who became a mother early in life, I would tell other young moms this: listen to those who are older and stable. Don't worry about being your children's friend; be the parent. Discipline your children instead of just letting them do whatever they want and thinking the stuff they do is cute. It may be cute when they're little, but they won't be little forever. Teach them respect and responsibility; how to clean, wash the dishes, make their beds, clean their rooms; and be resourceful.

:::::

As an adult, I realized the importance of forgiveness. So when my mother made choices that I didn't always agree with, I still tried always to be there whenever she needed me.

My mom didn't give any advice about motherhood that I took to heart—at least nothing that stands out or nothing I remember. We bonded in other ways, such as going on shopping trips and talking about TV shows over the phone. I realized as I matured that people have their own ways of expressing love, and my mother loved me a great deal.

In my adult years, my mom and I did a lot together. We often sat on the phone while watching the same beauty pageant on TV, such as *Miss America*, and talked about the program, judging what the dresses looked like and who would win. My mother also went with me to the local flea markets and rummage sales because we loved to shop. She accompanied me at church services, too.

My mother passed away suddenly in July of 1992. At the time, my third child was two years old. I was in a state of shock when I heard that my mom had died instantly in a car accident, where my sister, Evelyn, sustained serious injuries.

In retrospect, I feel as though I took my mother's last breath.

The night of her death, a childhood friend and I went out partying in Flint, Michigan. Once I got home, I laid down on my waterbed. I felt so sick! It was like I wanted to throw up, but I couldn't bring up anything. I fell asleep, then woke up again. I went to the bathroom to try to throw up; when I returned to bed, I placed the garbage can next to my bed. Suddenly, I let out a big gasp before finally rolling over and going to sleep. It turns out that this happened during the exact time of the accident.

Somehow, I coped with my grief in the following months. I didn't really have any strategies or activities that helped me through that time. Every day was difficult.

Around this time, my sister, Evelyn, put her energy into co-founding the nonprofit organization Women of Colors (WOC). I participated in some of WOC's projects.

I enjoyed WOC because it is community-oriented and service-oriented. I connected with other women and mothers who participated. The sense of community has done a lot for me and bonding with women from different walks of life. Women from diverse cultural, occupational, and socioeconomic backgrounds get together to promote the common good, which is serving the community and helping other people.

::::::

I adopted three children after becoming a foster parent in my early twenties. My aunt Lorean suggested that I would make a good foster parent; I babysit for her when she fostered kids. I see very little difference between being an adoptive mother versus being a biological mother to my children. You treat them all the same. In fact, you actually have to love your adopted kids more because of what they go through in being afraid and being away from a familiar household. They need extra love from their adoptive parents. No matter how much you provide for them, how good their life is, or how much love you give them, they still desire their biological mother and family regardless of the situation or circumstances.

I took a few things from my aunt about how to raise a family. But the most important one is this: love your foster children, make sure they're cared for, and treat them like they're your own. Nurture your mother-child relationship until they feel like part of the family.

With so many children to provide for, I worked hard. The majority of my former jobs were labor-intensive, except for Visiting Angels, a home healthcare service. At one time, I had three jobs, one full-time and two part-time, and I was trying to go to school to learn medical billing. Soon after I added the full-time job to my plate, I had to let school go. I was just getting good at medical billing—I was finally catching on to what I was doing— but I thought, "I have all these kids, so I need to make sure we have enough money coming in." I decided to focus on my jobs and put school on hold.

Because my children were involved in sports and extracurricular activities, I wanted to be available for them during the afternoons and evenings. For the majority of jobs I had, except for the post office, I worked the third shift so that I could be more engaged in their daytime lives and secure a babysitter to watch my kids at night.

:::::

Like all mothers, I have my strengths and weaknesses. My biggest strength is that I love hard. I love and am a strong believer in family. Sometimes I can sense that my strengths and weaknesses as a mother changed from my teens, when I raised my first three children, to my twenties, when I raised my adopted children. Overall, though, I believe my parenting style was relatively consistent between both experiences. As I matured, I became more lenient with my kids in some areas and firmer in others.

As a mother, I am committed, resourceful, and nurturing. I'm ready to die for my kids, but I hold them accountable—if they're doing wrong, they're doing wrong. While my biological and adopted sons—a total of six boys—were young, I offered a voice of reason and a listening ear, but I respected that they had to make their own decisions—they had to make their own choices. Looking at other people's children, I think it's important to have somebody you can talk to and relate with as a child, a mother figure who will discuss issues with you in a loving and nonjudgmental way.

I communicated openly with my sons when they were growing up. I didn't really keep my feelings from them. If I hurt, I let them know I hurt. If things were good, I let them know what was good so they wouldn't take it for granted. It's important to let your children know the reality of life; that people and things aren't always going to be fair, and that life is not a bed of roses; it's tough.

If I could change anything about the way I raised my sons, I would have talked to my children more about personal matters. I wish it had been easier for them to come to me and start a conversation, and they had felt more comfortable talking to me about anything.

I still play a key role in my children's adult lives because I try to keep up! I try to stay in constant contact with my children. We grew up together—that's how I look at it—given that I was so young when I became a mother. I try to stay updated on my sons' lives now that they have grown up, and when the family gets together, we always have a good time.

:::::

I use a daily mindfulness practice that helps with grounding and reflection. My morning routine is inspired by my dad, who used to study the Word, read his Bible, and pray first thing in the morning.

As soon as I wake up, even if I'm still lying down, I go to *Our Daily Bread* and read the passage they have for the day. I then read any scriptures connected with the passage and pray. That's how I start my day! If I'm ever not able to follow this routine in the morning, I make sure to do so before the day is over.

Everything changes when I start my day like that. The Word prepares me for what I may have to deal with during that day. I have a foundation or basis to deal with whatever's coming.

I send the *Our Daily Bread* passage to my kids daily. Once I finish reading it, I send it to them. I believe one of them reads it on a consistent basis. Because my dad inspired me with his spiritual practice, I want to pass it down to the next generation.

::::

I have raised my family with some of the same values and practices handed down from my mom. For example, I liked to dress my sons nicely and neat for gatherings at Easter and other holidays. Even though I didn't live with my mother during the second half of my childhood, she instilled values in her children that, to this day, have helped me navigate my life. She taught me, "Just be yourself. You can do the best you can, but just be yourself."

If Mom were living and I had the opportunity to tell her something today, I would say that I miss her and her wit. And I'm sorry that I couldn't do it when she asked me to give her a pedicure. That's the only thing I regret—that I didn't do her feet.

My advice to other women is not to rush into or through motherhood. Don't hurry to become a mother, but once you do, make your children your priority because their childhood is eighteen-plus years, and you still have a lifetime for other things once they move out. For those eighteen-plus years, you're responsible for them. So you've got to take care of them: How you treat them—and how you raised them—in my opinion, is going to reflect on you sooner or later when they get older.

Don't put any man or any dog before your children. I say that because a lot of mothers do that these days. Take care of yourself—that way, you can take care of your children—but don't put a bunch of material stuff before your children. Your relationship with your children is important.

My sons and I have a good relationship now. Value your relationship with your family, especially your parents and your kids. Love them, don't judge them, because we all have a story, and we all have a past. None of us are perfect; we've all made mistakes. As you go through life, try putting yourself in someone else's shoes, and look at it as if your life could be better or worse!

::::::

I am close with my sons to this day. I try to talk to them all the time. We use a group text to stay in touch on a daily or weekly basis, depending on how busy they are.

I have taught my children some good lessons about life:

- Stick with family, stay close and value family! We are all leaving here pretty quickly, so it's important to stay in touch and stay close.
- Slow down, don't be in a hurry to go or do, because whatever you have to do, or wherever you are going, it's going to be there whether you make it there or not.

- Be careful whom you reference as family and/or friends because some people don't mean you any good; some people are only in your life for a reason and/or a season.

- Every so often, take some time to sit, meditate, and do an inventory of your own life.

- Say what you want to say to a person; tell them how you really feel. Be honest with them because you just never know how much time you have left on this earth.

:::::

My chosen verse for this book reminds me to stay close to family because tomorrow is not a promise. Your tomorrow could be today.

I've always been family-oriented. Unfortunately, it seems as though people today don't value life like they used to, and they don't value family either. People are growing apart and becoming more disconnected. They are putting other priorities before family time. But family is going to be there in good times and bad times, so you need to stay close to them. If you've got any bad blood, it's important to work it out before it's too late.

:::::

Why, you do not even know what will happen tomorrow. What is your life? You are a mist that appears for a little while and then vanishes (James 4:14 *NIV*).

SANDRA'S MOTHER:

Sandra's Mother, Dorothy Mae Ledbetter

Sandra and Mother

Left to Right (Sandra, Mom, Evelyn)

ABOUT THE AUTHOR:

Social Media:
Email wootensandra@hotmail.com

Sandra Wooten, age 59, is the mother of six sons (three biological and three adopted). She was a foster and adoptive parent for fifteen years. Sandra grew up the youngest of four siblings and is the only sister of Evelyn McGovern.

Sandra has held many jobs, including city seasonal employee, US post office seasonal employee, Dow Event Center concession worker, DHS employee, night manager for Flying J / Pilot Truck Stop, Board Secretary for Women of Colors, and she frequently volunteered at the Community Action Center in Saginaw, MI. She also studied Medical Billing/Coding and Law Enforcement. Her hobby is spending time with family.

THE MOTHER MARCIA KNOWS
Marcia Reeves

When I think about how to characterize my mother, the first word that comes to my mind is strong. However, I don't know a word that fully describes her personality. She was bold and outgoing yet somewhat introverted. I could never truly read her; she always seemed deep in thought. I often wondered if she was reflecting on the cares of the world.

My mother was twenty years old and unmarried when she had me. Our family dynamics reflected a happy household. I am my mother's middle child, born after my older sister and before my younger brother.

I was very close to my mother. I was close to her because I carry a lot of her personality traits like her sense of humor, shopping, and enjoying family. Like my mother, I like to be around a lot of family too; I love being around my cousins at family events. I think that's why she and I were close, especially in her latter years. She filled a best friend role when I was navigating adulthood. But in my younger years, my mother probably had more interaction with my older sister than she did with me, giving her more household responsibilities. My mother didn't really teach me domestic skills like she taught my sister.

Mom lost her mother when she was eleven, so her childhood and adolescence were filled with a lot of pain. When she got pregnant with my sister, my mother decided to drop out of high school. Again, she didn't have her own mother in her life when she became a teen mother. I think Mom spent a lot of time reflecting on her life, such as, "Maybe I could have been more ahead had I not decided to stop attending school." Life was hard for a single mom getting off welfare and trying to make it.

I took all the cooking and cleaning my mom did for me for granted until I became a mother. The number-one thing is that we had to defrost a refrigerator to clean it back in the day. My mother and my sister took care of that chore for our household, so when I finally got on my own, I did not know how to defrost a refrigerator. I also wish my mother would have taught me how to make gravy. She made the best gravy. My first gravy was a hot mess; it was straight-up flour and water!

I don't think my mother treated her children any differently as far as love. But she groomed each of us for different roles. For example, my mother groomed my sister to be domestic. My mother needed help in the household because she was a single mom with a job. Justifiably she wanted to groom my sister to help her with cooking and cleaning. No one person can do everything, so my mother had to teach my sister how to take on a woman's responsibilities. This arrangement was mutually beneficial because my sister learned to do things that would help her run her own home one day.

In adulthood, I started to put two and two together about those quiet moments. As I mentioned, I used to see my mother deep in thought when I was a little girl. I would be playing or doing my homework, and then I would look over at her sitting on the couch, as if in a different world. She was a single mom with three children, and she had a lot to worry about each day. Although she may have started out struggling and on the welfare system, by the time she died, life had turned around, and she did some amazing things.

From what I understand, my mother and my aunt were academically gifted students, but when Mom got pregnant, she didn't complete her education. She had to come back around to confront that area of her life. My mother went back to school, earned her GED, and attended Rutgers University in New Jersey. At this time, my older sister was already a teenager, so she was able to take care of herself, but my brother and I went to an after-school program while my mother attended classes. I think it was similar to Michigan Works (job placement program), where they help moms get back on their feet. Thanks to this program, we had a place to go after school. A bus picked my younger brother and me up and took us to the YMCA.

Mom worked very hard, and she worked all her life. After taking classes, she got her first solid job in a hospital as a payroll clerk. She did so well that she became the payroll supervisor, and by the time of her death, she was the payroll manager, where she managed the executive payroll for all doctors. In 1984, she was named Employee of the Year. My mother may not have graduated from high school, but she was always smart.

I watched my mother go to work every day as a little girl. Even before she got the job at St. Joseph's, she took factory jobs. Once she went back to school and got training in data processing, that's when she got the payroll position at St. Joe's, which was like working at Covenant Health Care Center or St. Mary's Hospital. Watching her go to work every day gave me my work ethic because she never called in sick. Even at my mother's death, she had nearly two months of sick and vacation time; she always went to work. Thankfully, I've never had to rely on the welfare system and have always had a job.

I got a lot out of just watching her life. Even my relationship with God, I owe to her because I saw my mother's life shift when she surrendered to God and started going to church. When she started taking us to church, not sending us to church, our lives started to change. She eventually married a loving and supportive husband.

By the time I came along, my mother wanted someone to accompany her on grocery runs. She wanted me to be her roadie, her buddy to go places. So, as a little girl, I went along if she had to go downtown or go to the grocery store. She didn't have a car in the early years, but we would jump on the bus. That's when I started to hang out with her.

In my childhood, I didn't mind going grocery shopping. In fact, as we got older, that became our thing to do. My mother knew how much I liked fashion, and she enjoyed it when I shopped for her on

Mother's Day—I would usually buy her an outfit. She always looked forward to whatever I would buy because she liked my taste. One of the last things we did before she died was go shopping together.

I knew my mother loved us because she protected us. She was very careful about where she would let us go and picky about the people, she would allow us to be around, even if they were family. Of course, as kids, we questioned her decisions sometimes. I thought, "But why can't we do this?" Finally, she would explain her reservations upfront: "No, I don't want you going over to so-and-so's house because I don't know who else lives over there."

Even though my mother didn't have a lot, she did small things to show how much she cared about us. She made sure our hair was always done and that we were neat and clean. She took us to barbecues with our cousins. Even though my father wasn't in my home, she would let me go and spend time with him. So, that was my love language. That's what made me feel loved. But my mother never said it until I was an adult—she never was the type that would say, "I love you." But when I was a little girl, she would affirm me. She would say, "Well, don't you look pretty today?"

I absolutely feel that my mother loved me. I experienced a traumatic accident at the tender age of three-and-a-half, so I saw that love early on. I was severely burned when my mother accidentally dropped scalding hot water on me. I went through a horrific time in the hospital and then, of course, growing up with the scars. I didn't even want to wear short sleeves or shorts as a little girl. Maybe in those pockets of time when my mother was in deep thought, the accident could have even been on her mind. She carried that burden with her, too. In my feature film *Sunshine Circle*, I pay homage to my mother for her strength and our resiliency in enduring that tragedy.

My mother has said, "I love you" to me a thousand times without saying it aloud. One example of her motherly love still stands out to me. When I was in first grade, a classmate of mine got killed—that was another one of my childhood traumas—but I'll never forget what my mother did for me. I was sitting on the couch, just waiting for her to come home from work, and when she came in, I ran and grabbed her leg. I was crying. She said, "What happened?" I said, "Gladys died." I explained through tears that my friend had gotten hit while crossing a street.

My mother took me to her viewing. She held my hand and walked me to the funeral home so that I could pay my last respects to Gladys. It was a good little walk. When I look back now, I think that was such an amazing thing for my mother to do. I was so distraught at six years old; I was grieving about my friend dying. So, for my mother to do that—was so big of her.

I'll never forget Gladys was inside a white coffin with a pretty pink chiffon dress. I remember just being at peace after I saw Gladys because she looked so pretty. I wish I could have told my mother how much that meant to me, but you don't fully appreciate it when you're young. I wish my mother were living for me to tell her how much I look back and realize the closure I got as a little girl because I got to see my friend one last time. My mother didn't have a lot, but those were the ways she did a lot with a little.

I counted it an honor that I grew up with the mother I had. During my growing-up years, I saw friends whose mothers had died, and it just troubled me. I would be so sad knowing that somebody lost their mother because I could never imagine life without mine. My mother was my protector. She took us to the doctor and made sure of this and that. Looking back, I feel so grateful for a mother's hand in my life. My relationship with my mother was mostly without conflict; however, we faced challenges in our relationship when I was coming of age and wanted to have boyfriends. I got pregnant early in life at nineteen. I was still living at home, and my mother and I got into a conflict because she let me know that she was not going to babysit. I moved out, and I hurt her—I hurt her deeply—when I left.

Once I was out of the house, we started to rebuild our relationship, not that it was completely torn apart. My first son was born premature, so my mother was concerned about me being on my own at nineteen with a premature baby. But once she saw that I could take care of myself, she supported my decision, and we got past our differences.

My mother instilled many values in me. One of the values that I love is that she really believed in self-care because, as a single mother, she was determined to enjoy life. After she got over the breakup of her last boyfriend, she was not going to let life be dependent on a relationship with a man. So, she stopped dating. She got rooted and grounded in the Word of God, and she started to travel and do things for herself. I always admired her for going to the Bahamas with her friends; she even went once by herself. My mother believed in taking care of herself and rewarding herself for working so hard. I followed my mother's example and traveled too as a young lady. I was a single mom at the time, but I made sure I did things for my son and me.

I love my mother for setting an example for me. I got a lot out of just watching her life. Even my relationship with God, I owe to her because I saw my mother's life shift when she surrendered to God and started going to church. When she started taking us to church, not sending us to church, our lives started to change. She eventually married a loving and supportive husband.

My mother was also big on Mother's Day. I wonder if maybe she made such a big deal out of the holiday because she lost her mother at a young age. We would always have a really special time on that holiday. It was a fun event where we had a family get-together, and sometimes we went to a restaurant. I have always wanted to put on a Mother's Day celebration as my mother did, but it has fallen short every year.

My mother died at age fifty-one. If she were living and I had the opportunity to tell her something today, I would definitely say thank you. And I would have to say that I still had to respect her decisions—some of them good, some of them not so good. I would tell my mother how proud she made me. When I look at her going back to school, traveling, and becoming an Employee of the Year for a hospital that had 2,800 employees—I feel proud to be her daughter.

To be a mother means everything to me. I could be honest to say I only wanted boys. I didn't want any girls because I knew what

I was like as a girl. I thought, "You know what? I don't want any daughters." God honored my wish, and I only have boys, and I tell you, I love them! There's a family saying in my home that I literally am the queen of the house because my two boys and my husband protect and spoil me.

Motherhood is an honor that a woman gets to have in life. To be able to bear children, watch children grow, and then later have your children become your best friends is a beautiful thing. It's amazing just to be a mom to me. My mother was strong, intelligent, and wise. As a mother to my two sons, who are seventeen years apart in age, I consider myself to be fun, transparent, and compassionate. I've experienced motherhood on both sides. I've been a single mother, and I've been a mother with the support of a husband; both experiences (of being a mom to my sons) have been good for me.

As a mother, I never experienced any real conflict between my boys and me. That said, like every other mother, I had to learn that my sons are different from each other. They had different styles, so I had to learn that and how to deal with them as individuals, especially with that much of an age gap. It came up in different areas and different hobbies. My younger son wanted to get into sports and music, but my older son liked to read comic books. It was a process of learning and coming to terms with what each of my sons enjoyed so that I could treat them as individuals.

I almost made the mistake of showing partiality between my sons—but I caught myself— because I realized my boys learned differently. My older son was very independent. He liked to complete his homework on his own, and as a single mom, I was happy; I let him be independent. On the other hand, my younger son wanted to have more affirmation about different things that he did when it came to school. I found myself saying, "Oh, just go ahead, you can do it," pushing him to be independent, too. And then one day, I got the revelation: "Okay, he's not his brother. He wants more. He wants me to sit at the table with him doing homework." While my older son preferred to go off to his room, do what was assigned, turn it in, and come back saying, "Mom, I got an A," my younger son liked having that intimate time with his parents.

I mimicked my mother as far as the liberties that she allowed me to have. She let me go to school dances, so I permitted them to do things like that. I was overprotective with my older son, who grew up in New Jersey with a bunch of cousins. My younger son didn't have any family in Saginaw, Michigan, so I tended to let him go to fewer places, but I still allowed him to do things when he was a bit older.

I don't think I have any habits that my mother did, but she practiced self-care and learned to enjoy life which has stuck with me. When I was a single mom, my son and I traveled, and we learned to do things despite what I was dealing with at the time. We learned to do things as a family, such as family reunions. My mother was responsible for coordinating the first family reunion with all her cousins. Family reunions were big when my mother was alive, and we still do them. I have continued the practice of staying in touch with our cousins. Like my mother, I gave my sons the best that I could. I introduced them to Christ, and I made sure they knew their family's importance.

I would tell other mothers to treat their children as individuals based on their personalities and temperaments. Enjoy them while you have them with you because one day you look up, and they will be grown. Save all your pictures. Now that so many phones function as cameras take in the moment and capture it so you have something to go back and look at at any time. I'm so happy that I still have stuff that my boys gave me. I have a whole file drawer with awesome stuff—school projects that they did, report cards, etc.

I am grateful that I witnessed the shift in our home when my mother surrendered her life to the Lord and committed to her walk of faith. Likewise, I am grateful that both of my boys were introduced to Christ and witnessed my faith in Christ. I am grateful that they saw hardship and good times; it made us all stronger.

"Charm is deceitful, and beauty is passing, but a woman who fears the Lord, she shall be praised" (Proverbs 31:30).

MARCIA'S MOTHER:

Marcia's Mother, Carrie Wise

EMPLOYEE OF THE YEAR - Carris Wise, left, displays Employee of the Year aw
resented by Sister Jane at 24th Annual Employee Awards Dinner, which also hon
wenty Year Club retirees and those in the Twenty Year Club, Fifteen Year Club
n Year Club.

Marcia's Mother receiving Employee of the Month award

ABOUT THE AUTHOR:

Social Media:
Email sunshinec1964@gmail.com

Marcia Michelle Reeves was born in Paterson, New Jersey. She attended Paterson Public Schools, including graduating from Eastside High, featured in the movie *Lean on Me*. Raised by a single mother, Marcia says her childhood, although faced with tragedy, was good. She enjoyed fashion, being creative, and spending time with friends. Her vivid imagination inspired her to coordinate her first Performing Arts event at the age of twelve.

Michelle moved to Michigan in 1992 to attend Mid-Michigan Teen Challenge, a program for individuals battling life issues. The program helped her address childhood trauma and overcome a seven-year of drug addiction. In 1993, she joined New Covenant Christian Center Church, where she led teens and supported individuals overcoming addiction. In 1998, she became Ministry of the Arts director, an assignment she still fulfills.

Marcia is a published poet, playwright, screenwriter, choreographer, and more. She is the Public Relations Director and Administrative Assistant for the largest homeless care provider in mid-Michigan.

Named Woman of the Year in 2014 by the Saginaw Zeta Phi Beta Sorority, she was recognized by the State of Michigan, the City of Saginaw, and the Saginaw County Commissioners. In 2017, she received the Multicultural Arts grant from the State of Michigan. Marcia is passionate about sharing her story. She has been featured in the Hope Is Real documentary, on the Big Impact podcast, and Total Christian Television. She is happily married and the mother of two adult sons. Marcia is the screenwriter and producer of her independent film, "Sunshine Circle."

THE MOTHER LULA KNOWS
Lula R. Woodard

My mother, Doris Bernice (Eddins) Williams, was the only girl out of three brothers and became the mother of seven children. I saw my mom as a hard worker and a disciplinarian at times. Nevertheless, she instilled in us to work, play, get an education, and help everyone.

My mom and dad, Joseph Williams Jr., got married on Christmas Day in 1945 when they were in their twenties. I was born in 1948 and was the oldest of seven children. My mom and my dad both worked. Often, I had the responsibility to supervise my younger siblings because after my mom got off work at the University of Alabama, she was also a beautician. Mom had a great work ethic. You don't have much time for other activities when working multiple jobs as she did.

I spent a lot of time playing outside with my brothers and sisters in Tuscaloosa, Alabama. I tried to stay out of the house, where I wouldn't be in the way because my mother did hair inside our home.

Customers were always in our place, so I guess you could say there was some hospitality there. Hospitality is a thread that runs through our family.

My mom sent my siblings and me to church regularly. Sometimes she went with us; other times, we attended services with my dad's brothers and sisters because they lived near us. As a result of having a huge family on my dad's side, my childhood friendships mostly involved family interaction. I had so many siblings and cousins that I didn't need any other friends. Dad was the seventh child of eleven, in which were born my sixty-four first cousins; fifty-four is still with us today.

My daily life changed dramatically at age eleven when my mother sent me to live with my grandparents, who then raised me. My mother explained that I was the oldest child, so she thought it would be better for me to live with my grandparents in Chicago than for one of my brothers or sisters.

After I transitioned from my mom's to my grandmother's home, I planned visits with my mom and siblings. At this point, my dad had left their household. My parents had separated, so he lived in their birth city of Aliceville, Alabama, with his mom, my Big Mama Lula, due to having gone blind without any medical evidence. After six months, he regained sight and restored life activities but never returned to our house. So, when I would go for summer vacation from Chicago, I would spend time with my mom in her house, but I would also spend time with my dad in his mother's house, later in his own rural home.

Later, I realized just how much my dad and grandmother loved me in my childhood. I used to hang out with my dad when he got off work and worked on cars. He became a self-made mechanic, and we built a 1954 Chevy, which amazed me. I found out what love was all about from my grandmother by setting goals, saving money, family, and increased spirituality, along with fun.

Remember, my childhood lasted up until age eleven. I was about to hit adolescence when I moved across Alabama to Chicago. I spent my adolescent years through young adulthood with my grandmother.

As I grew into adulthood, I had to transition to my grandmother's household and be away from my biological mother. This experience had a profound impact on my life. I questioned then and now, why was I the one sent to live with my grandparents? At first, I found it challenging to manage my expectations because of the drastic nature of the transition. I went from a young mom to grandparents in their fifties and from Tuscaloosa to Chicago.

My lifestyle was different when I went to Chicago because I had never encountered racial or cultural diversity in Tuscaloosa. When I was young, every person I saw was Black or white. I didn't see Hispanic/Latinos, Asians, or people who spoke different languages until I moved to Chicago. With time, I developed strategies for managing this transition. One thing that helped is that I am a bookworm. So, I decided that I would learn as much and read as many books as possible about different people and places.

In the community where I lived with my grandparents, we had Puerto Rican neighbors and white neighbors and integrated schools.

I came from a segregated school of all-Black teachers and students, but my elementary school in Chicago was very diverse. I had white teachers, Black teachers, and various school administrators.

Luckily, my grandmother got me into church ministries such as Sunday school, choir, Red Circle, and Sunshine Band, and she got me involved with some of the youth programs; those kinds of things helped a lot in keeping me active and grounded.

After my baby brother passed away, my mom and siblings moved to Chicago, but we still lived in two different households. At one point, we lived in the same building in Chicago. They lived on the second floor, and I lived on the first floor with my grandparents. Sometimes I stayed with them on the weekends, and sometimes I didn't because my life had taken an entirely different trajectory from their lives.

Before I became a mother, the sense of family had been established in me and demonstrated by my mother's many vivid experiences which remain a part of my life and legacy. In Alabama, we had Fish Fry Friday, Saturday hangouts with the clan after chores were done, and on Sunday after church dinner attending the baseball game with family and extended family. These were my fond memories as a child. Therefore, it may seem odd that I would say family given that I didn't live with my parents and siblings as a teenager; however, I still had a big family during and beyond my adolescent years, even when I went to Chicago. Four of my dad's sisters reside in the city of Chicago with their families providing me with a tribe and support called my "cousin sisters and brothers," and they continue to help me thrive into becoming a mother.

Education was a critical value that my mother instilled in me. She believed in education and working to make a living. I saw her work ethic firsthand.

If my mother were living and I had the opportunity to tell her something today, first, I would say that I love her and that I know motherhood can be messy. It's challenging and involves a lot of craziness, many sleepless nights, and a lot of giving of yourself. And there is beauty in all of that. But, when I step back and take a mature look at my childhood, I realize that my mother did the best that she could with the information and resources that she had available. It wasn't easy raising my siblings. It would have been much more difficult raising four girls and two boys by herself.

As I mentioned, my younger brother passed away when he was four months old from Sudden Infant Death Syndrome or SIDS, as I know now. I was home in Tuscaloosa, Alabama, when my brothers and sisters were born. Still, I don't remember much about my mother's pregnancy and postpartum experiences, other than my aunts coming to help her out after she had the babies. When I was growing up, kids were not privy to that information and didn't get involved in those matters. Whatever the adults did, that's what they did. Kids wouldn't hear grown folks' conversations, much unlike today's children.

:::::

I got married at age nineteen to my children's father, L. C. Woodard, and we were together for fourteen years. To me, motherhood means being an unselfish mom because it's no longer about me; it's about the welfare of my children. I've dedicated my life to my two daughters, Sanora (the older) and Larissa (the younger).

A significant life challenge I faced was addiction. Although for some people who have experienced trauma, their emotional and life issues tend to surface when they get high, this was not the case for me. I walked in silence, but it was a cover-up. Everything was okay, even though things were not okay. I put on a mask to cover my psychological, social, and emotional issues.

By age forty-five, I never imagined becoming a full-blown alcoholic and addict from drinking socially in my early twenties. So, I dealt with my addiction in silence for a long time. However, I eventually sought treatment for my addiction and alcoholism, which led me to therapy for several years to help with my recovery, personal issues, family, chronic stress, trauma, and even depression.

I hope my children remember me as a humble, helpful, loving God, a servant, a lifelong learner, and a spiritual mother. I truly knew that my grandmother loved me because she hugged me, told me, and showed me. She demonstrated to me what love looks like, and that's what I did for my daughters when they were growing up, as far as taking them to church and showing them love in many ways. It wasn't just a verbal thing. I touched them, hugged them, and listened to them—and I still do the same thing today. As a result, I'm engaging in their lives.

Clinically speaking, I was a functioning alcoholic and addict. Coming out of denial and admitting that you have a problem is vital for a mother suffering from alcoholism or addiction. I had to admit that I had a problem and that my life was unmanageable, but I couldn't see that part because I thought I was teaching my girls financial and homemaking skills. I was taking them to games and was there for them. I would also tell a functionally addicted mother to cultivate a great support system. I ended up having a great support system and still do today; I call them my tribe. I would tell her that it's okay not to be okay. Most important, develop a relationship with God and a prayer life.

Affirmations are powerful. I don't use them as much as I used to, but at one point, I used them daily because they began to bring me into who I am. And I just know that my grandmother always knew—because she was a Christian, a missionary, a praying woman—that I would turn the curve and pivot to be okay because God answers prayer.

My grandmother was loving, caring, and a disciplinarian. She didn't just see me as her granddaughter but more like her daughter, and she treated me as such. My grandmother (my grandma) wanted to see me succeed academically, financially, and spiritually. So she put me into Charm School for girls. She made sure that I had a great spiritual inheritance. I would tell my grandmother that her spiritual inheritance has meant a lot to me; my spiritual life is so important because of how she prayed. I watched her go into a room by herself and listen to her pray. I went to church with her and saw our needs met through prayer. My grandmother retired after thirty years as a housekeeper at Wesley Memorial Hospital in Chicago. Then after retiring, she returned to volunteer at the hospital for several years. Maybe that's where I developed a heart for volunteerism.

Despite my addiction and her not seeing my recovery journey, I know that she knew deep in her heart that the person she raised would come out of it. She knew that I would be a role model for other women, grandmothers, mothers, children, grandchildren, and great-grandchildren—because of her. I owe my grandmother a debt of gratitude and honor for taking me on because she didn't have to do it. She could have been terrible; some grandmothers treat their grandkids horribly, but that's not my story. My story is that my grandmother taught me how love looked. She touched me. She held me. I called her my Jet Set grandmother because wherever you saw me, you saw her; wherever you saw her, you saw me.

My grandmother took me on many trips. She taught me to pre-plan for her funeral, how to budget, and home economics. All these things made me the woman I am today. Because of her and what she instilled in me through the years, I am becoming. She would always tell me, "I don't want any of your money. I just want you to go to school, get a good education, and give back." And that's what I did. That's what I'm doing. I owe that to her. So, this is my tribute to her and other grandparents and parents: No matter how low the low points in life, believe there is hope and light on the other side.

I am named after my grandmothers: my dad's mother, Lula Williams, and my mother's mother, Rosa Eddins. Mistakenly, I got the "e" instead of the "a" from her in "Rose." I didn't like my name growing up, but now it reminds me of two powerful Black American women in my life whom I adore and appreciate. These women helped shape the woman that I'm becoming. And I'm still becoming.

::::

It's challenging being a mother. You must be able to look adversity in the eye and say, "I can overcome these things." But a lot of it you just can't do by yourself, so you must have a tribe, a person, or a group of people there to help you—many mothers today attempt to do it by themselves, causing problems for themselves and their children. Especially with substance use and addiction, you can't get over addiction by yourself. Rarely can one do that; some have, but not very often. A person must receive help by asking for it when needed. Denial is your enemy; so is pridefulness.

One must know that motherhood is not a bed of roses. When the baby grows up and becomes a teenager, they start getting inquisitive. Some babies want to check out the cigarettes, drinking, drugs, and sex. Life can be challenging for mothers because babies don't stay babies for long. That little bundle of joy starts walking and starts getting into stuff. It is my responsibility as a mother to teach spiritual-biblical principles and model good leadership character behavior in the school, community, church, relatives, and other venues. It is my belief that not enough family relationships are being developed between children and parents in today's society. The "Ten Commandments" in the Bible give us standards to live by and follow which are highly recommended. There is a 2022 epidemic in the United States and probably the world where kids are killing kids, people are killing kids, and adults are killing each other, causing mothers grief and uncertainty. If the Bible says, "Thou shalt not kill," then why is this happening? Because we are not teaching spiritual, biblical principles in our homes.

We've gotten away from many biblical principles that our churches taught in childhood. Looking back, I recall children were not allowed into adult conversations, but that's no longer the case. We've let the guards down in parenting and mothering. We have a lot of single parents, single mothers, grandparents, and great-grandparents who are raising these children because the mothers or fathers are not able to do so because of incarceration, human trafficking, drugs, or other issues. Parents/guardians must be purposeful and intentional with goals and strategies for the welfare of the child or children.

Having survived cancer, recovered from addiction and alcoholism, grieved the death of many loved ones, and experienced suicide attempts, near-death auto accidents, and my time in the Alabama National Guard, I've lived through a great deal. But I can say that I can overcome because of my faith and what my grandmother instilled in me.

I am proud of my role in my children's lives. I've shown my girls love, so they know how it looks. They'll tell you, "Hey, I love my mama." I allowed them to talk to me openly. I ask them, "How are you feeling?" "How was your day?" That means a lot to a kid. Let's go for a walk and get some ice cream. Let me see your report card and your progress report. Okay, let's focus on what's good and not good. Why is this? What can I do better? We've had those kinds of conversations.

Travel was also crucial in my adult family life. Their dad and I always took our children on vacations. We traveled around the United States to places such as Colorado Springs, Pikes Peak,

Garden of the Gods in Colorado, the Midwest, and many other states. We took our kids to fairs, parties, and swimming. We played games and did other activities within our family, along with the pets we loved. It was important to me that my children had these experiences growing up.

I got a weekly trip with my grandparents when I was growing up. Every Sunday after church, my grandmother and grandfather would take me for a drive in Chicago. As we were driving, I began to read the street names. I can still get around Chicago by street names! That's how they taught me to navigate living in Chicago, so I taught that to my girls. My daughters are great drivers. They've learned how to fix cars, too, because I instilled that in them. I learned how to take care of a car from watching my dad and several uncles who were self-educated mechanics and the group at the auto repair shop were all licensed mechanics. I am on this journey to love, serve, protect, teach, and be my daughter's grand, and great cheerleader! This is for and to the Mother I Know.

:::::

My younger daughter liked tap dancing, played piano, ran track, sang in the choir at church, and was part of the cheerleading team. My older daughter played softball, was on the Pom-Pom Squad, sang in the school and church choir, and enjoyed swimming. They both sang in the Saginaw District Choir. They are two different people, so they have two different personalities. As a mother, I honor those differences while still treating my daughters with equity as human beings.

I continued some but not all of my mother's habits and practices when raising my daughters. Everything I do is usually out of love with choices rather than reflex. And so again, my daughters are good mothers, hard workers, and selfless. They give of themselves and to others. They promote education and are spiritual. They have a spiritual inheritance. I'm proud that they love the Lord and are active in ministry. A lot of this transfers to them through my family legacy.

In response, I would share with other mothers that motherhood means being unselfish, being able to admit that you don't have all the answers, and being willing to ask for help. There is no perfect mother because there is no ideal human being.

Mothers must become aware that they are their children's first teachers. When pregnant with a child, you must be careful about what you watch, listen to, and put into your body. And even after you have given birth to the child, it is essential to repeat the same behaviors, including protecting their ears and eyes and being careful about what they put into their bodies. In addition to that, teach them about spirituality. It's not necessarily practicing a religion because religion is different from spirituality. I practice spirituality and religion; however, I think I'm more of a spiritual person.

I see evidence that the spirituality facet is missing from our society based on the number of people who have trouble apologizing or forgiving others. When I'm wrong, I can admit that I'm wrong. I have no problem doing that. I know how to say that I'm sorry. These are some things that mothers should teach their children: not to steal from other people, not to lie, and not to hold a grudge. Spirituality is a sentiment that you should treat others the way you want to be treated. Furthermore, if I don't want to be harmed or lied to, then I'm not going to do that to you. Unfortunately, we are not teaching today's kids spirituality or biblical principles. Many of them have heard it, but they haven't seen it put into practice. This generation is the third to the fifth generation of children and families who do not attend church regularly and are not involved in practicing spirituality and biblical teaching.

As life goes on, I seem to get farther away from the dead but have lasting memories. I've only been to my grandmother's gravesite in Tuscaloosa, Alabama, twice, and she's been dead since 1987. My mom passed away on Christmas Day in 1989. I've been to her gravesite in Chicago, Illinois, twice; the second time, I had just gotten out of treatment in 1993, and I brought a letter that I had written to her gravesite. I read the long letter, which discussed our mother-daughter relationship. In the last couple of pages, I told her how much I did love her. I think that gave me a sense of closure around our relationship (although Mother's Day is more emotional for me some years than others due to the loss of both my grandma and mama).

I want to leave my family with many legacies—a spiritual legacy, an educational legacy, a financial legacy, and a legacy around volunteerism. I just had a conversation with my two daughters about legacy. I want them, their children (Anea, Ayla, and Willie), and their children's children to know I may not be able to leave you a lot of money, but I'll leave you a few dollars. What I want to see is your spiritual development. I want you to have a relationship with God. I want you to be able to get a good education.

That doesn't necessarily mean a college degree, but get some type of education where you can take care of yourself and your future family.

If you get married, make sure you're careful about the person you marry. Ask, "Is God in their life? How does he treat his mother? How does she treat her father?" Look at what their life looks like because you're not just marrying them; you're marrying their family as well. If you should remain single, live a single life, and live the words of God. Enjoy living single.

It's important to talk about issues and not be secretive about your life. There's nothing wrong with acknowledging issues. It's okay to say that you're not okay. Be open to having conversations about the family's medical problems. Let your kids know about the family history and patterns. Maybe you've got a mother, father, or family member who has hypertension, diabetes, substance use disorder, depression, and other illnesses. Maybe cancer runs in the family. We talk about these subjects in the family so there can be preventive measures and interventions down the road, including my new granddaughters, Brittney and Regine, and my new son-in-love, Jarvis, all through marriage.

Besides that, be an active listener. Be a lifelong learner. Give to others and the community, which is huge because it makes you feel better when you give and help others. Finally, if you need to go into therapy or counseling, there's nothing wrong with it. For so long, people of color have denied the importance of treatment or counseling. The buzzword was, and often is, "If you go to therapy, you must be crazy." The truth is, that therapy or counseling gives you another arm of support or advocacy.

I'm "GG" to my amazing, lovable, intelligent great-grandchildren, Khloe, Ayden, Taylor, and Christopher." I appreciate talking to them, showing them love, and praying with them (and they do the same with me); adults didn't speak to children nearly as much in my childhood. I have a Saturday phone date with my oldest great-grandson, Ayden, who will be nine in August. We've had this date for five years. He recently got his mobile phone and is learning to text, so he texts me, "Hi, GG. Call me," before our date. I always look forward to that text and our conversations.

This child's grandfather, Pastor Howard, and his grandmother, lovingly called Yaya, attend their church with my great-grandson weekly, so my great-grandson goes to church regularly, getting that spiritual teaching. I pray with him over the phone, and he can pray with me back. Those are the kinds of things that I want to see thriving in my family when I'm no longer here. Ideally, I want to see some of it before I leave earth. And that's my prayer: that God will allow me to see some of this legacy. I believe He will grant it, and there's also longevity in my family because I have three living aunts (my dad's sisters) in Chicago. Josie Smith is ninety-six years old; Martha Williams is ninety-four years old. Genola Williams, who lives in Cleveland, is eighty-eight years old. They love the Lord.

I receive so much love and appreciation from my family. My daughters are amazing! I appreciate them for all that they do. I believe in my granddaughters the way my grandmother believed in me. I'm praying for them, and I know I can get a prayer through. I love my only grandson, Willie, and encourage him to pray, stay grounded, and ask for help when needed with assertiveness, along with the help of his wife, Brittney.

This past January marked forty-one years of living in Saginaw, Michigan. People in the community respect me today. And I was appreciated back when I struggled with and recovered from functional addiction, too—I just hadn't realized how much. Some people support me, who I thought had turned their backs on me because of my substance abuse. I found out that they were willing to accept me with open arms, and I'm appreciative of that. It means that I have to get over myself and forgive myself. I am still working on it because I must overcome those issues: People will forgive you, but forgiving yourself is vital. And some days I do; some days I don't. But it's better on this side. Every day is a good day. I've found hope by hearing other people's experiences, just as I can give hope to others by sharing my experiences—along with biblical scriptures to incorporate into their lives.

My sistah-friends Mytris, Barbara, Kori, Doris, Claudia, Lynn, and Evelyn—amazing mothers—are my inner circle. I thank them for their support, kindness, friendship, prayers, and unconditional love for me.

I often ask myself, what can I pass on? I have noticed some parallels between my upbringing with my grandmother and my relationship with my two granddaughters. I showed them how love looks. I hug them, and I kiss them today; they're grown. I still do that because that's what my grandmother did for me. I took them to church. They were in the children's ministry and youth ministry. I'm always talking to my granddaughters about setting goals, managing money, education, spirituality, developing a relationship with God, and helping others along the way. So I'm transferring to them and my grandson and GG babies, those skills that my grandmother passed down to me.

My world is exploding with expansion. It's unbelievable that people embrace and acknowledge me, even to me at times. I just would not have dreamed in a million years of being where I am or even living this long. But what's impressive is that I haven't stopped at the age of seventy-two. If anything, I've just begun. My daughters call me the "Energizer Bunny" and tell their friends, "Our mother puts us to shame with all she is doing." Well, God has been and is truly good to me.

I stand on this scripture *"Being confident of this very thing: that He who began a good work in you will continue to perform it until the day of Jesus Christ."* (Philippians 1:6 [NIV]). And *"But those that wait upon the Lord, He shall renew their strength. They shall mount up with wings like eagles. They shall run and not be weary. They shall walk and not faint."* (Isaiah 40:31). I live my life based on those scriptures every day. I am living and walking them out. And so it says I haven't seen everything that the Lord has in store for me yet because I'm still becoming. I see myself as a light bearer and peacemaker in this world of uncertainty.

LULA'S MOTHER:

Lula's Mother, Doris Bernice (Eddins) Williams

Lula's Grandmother, Lula Williams

ABOUT THE AUTHOR:

Social Media:
Email lularwoodard2@yahoo.com

Lula R. Woodard is a proud mother of two, grandmother of five, and great-grandmother of four. She has resided in the City of Saginaw for over 41 years, relocating from her original home of Tuscaloosa, Alabama, and her second home of Chicago, Illinois.

Lula feels extremely passionate and compassionate about the field of education, community involvement, and social justice. She provides parenting sessions, coaching, facilitating, and mentoring through Women of Colors (WOC) in Saginaw, Michigan, and has been a member of this group for over twenty years. WOC awarded her Woman of the Year in 2012.

In WOC, Lula serves as a Prevention Specialist, facilitating the Botvin Life Skills and Prime for Life evidence-based programs. In addition, she became a Certified Recovery Coach to provide support as a resource or referral for individuals affected by substance abuse in the Great Lakes Bay Region.

Lula is a retired teacher, teacher consultant, social worker, and the Alabama National Guard member. She currently holds an Education Specialist degree in Education Leadership from Saginaw Valley State University and works as an Adjunct Professor in the English Division at Delta College. An aspiring entrepreneur, Lula expects to launch her business, Purposeful Intentional Parenting (PIP), which focuses on encouragement, empowerment, and skill-building for parents of teens ages twelve to fifteen years old.

Lula R. Woodward had received multiple awards and in 2022 she was awarded the Lynn Heatley Adjunct Service from Delta College for her excellent contributions to students' success. Her colleagues pointed out her extra efforts and wiliness to meet students' needs and help them remain critical to the program's success. She also received the Spirit of Dr. Martin Luther King, Jr. Award. In 2002, Ms. Woodward was awarded the Lynn Heatley Award for adjunct faculty distinguished services.

THE MOTHER VICKI KNOWS
Vicki Hill

My mother was a strong woman when it came to knowing how to take care of her family. One of her essential characteristics was resilience. She was adept at figuring out what she needed to do next and how she would provide for her children.

I was close to my mom. I was her oldest child who lived in Michigan, so I was the one that my mom always relied on the most. But, as a child, I didn't understand why my mother stayed and endured the different things she took in her marriage. My mom was an abused wife, so I did not know how she was able or willing to tolerate all the heartache, struggles, and pain that she went through in life.

As I got older, I understood to a point why she stayed. I realized that my mom could not work sometimes; she had medical conditions. In addition, my mother was not the breadwinner of the family and had no money to take care of all the children. She did not have the choice to walk out the door and leave and had to plan a strategy to prevent losing her life.

When my mother was with her first husband who abused her, I was five. After she divorced him, she had a boyfriend, so it was about a year before she met and married the man from church.

My mom has eight biological children: four boys and four girls. She was married twice. Her first husband, the father of four of her children, was an abuser. She got out of that marriage, and then she turned around and married another man she met in church. And little did she know she was entering the same situation all over again because she became an abused wife, which was much worse this time.

My mom's first husband was not a church-going man; I'm not sure where she met him. The second husband was a deacon who attended church every Sunday. He was downright evil in my eyes. My mother loved going to church so much that he would punish her by not allowing her to go to church anymore.

Neither one of these men is my father. I am the second of two children my mother had before her first marriage. Although technically I am the second child, I filled the role of the oldest child within our household because my big sister has lived in Spain since she graduated from high school. She aspired to go there and become a doctor. Instead, she ended up marrying someone of the Spaniard culture, and that's where she stayed; she did not live with us when I was growing up.

My childhood in my mother's household was tough. From five to thirteen or fourteen, my life was difficult when we finally got out of Benton Harbor, Michigan. At this time, my mom was married to her first husband. I remember all the bumps in the night, the crying, screams, and her trying to escape. I remember a whole lot of things.

As a child, I wasn't allowed to have friends. There were children in the home, so I was stuck babysitting or watching kids. Even though my mother was home to supervise my younger brothers and sisters, I wasn't allowed to go and play with my friends. I was only allowed to go to school and come home. I had this little sister who lied about me all the time, and as punishment, my stepfather locked me in my bedroom. So that's where I spent most of my time.

For a while, my mother worked a job in the flats in Benton Harbor. The flats were similar to the downtown area of Flint, Michigan, where their streets are brick. She worked the third shift.

My stepfather often came over when she was at work. I was home babysitting the rest of the kids because I was the oldest. My mom couldn't afford a babysitter, and we didn't have any family around at that particular time. My stepfather would knock on the door, and I would let him in the house because if I hadn't, he would get mad. He would wait for my mom to come home, and then he would beat her again.

Finally, my mother ended up getting a divorce from him. She had to seek somebody to watch us; of course, it's not safe to leave minor children at home by themselves. As the oldest child, I struggled to find something for the rest of my brothers and sisters to eat because we didn't have food. To keep them from starving, I would go to the kitchen and try to cook. I couldn't cook, but I had watched my mom, so I would try to figure out *something* just so that they weren't whining that their stomachs were empty, whether I ate anything or not. I was only five years old.

My mom decided to ask my cousin if she would allow her son to babysit us while she was working so he would not let my stepfather in the house.

My relationship with my mother differed from my sibling's relationship with my mother because they were young. Young children do what they do: Play, tear up houses, and mess up things. Given that I was the oldest, I watched the kids at age five and made sure that they stayed in line. And when they didn't stay in line or clean up the house, that was my responsibility. If they didn't do it correctly, I was punished for that—not necessarily by my mom but by my stepfather.

Although my mom had a callous life, she was still great in my eyes, and I didn't take anything my mother did for me for granted. She instilled many values in me that have played out in my adult life. For example, my mom taught me that I could be a strong woman by the standard. I watched her overcome a great deal of trauma and pain. She was strong, endured, and taught me how to be strong. My mom also showed me the importance of doing things for myself. She taught me to rely upon myself, not necessarily on a man to do or provide for me.

I believe my mom loved me. So I hear about mothers today— so many of them walk entirely away from their children. My mom could have done the same. She could have kept going and never returned—when she finally did escape—but she returned. My mom called me every day when she was gone to make sure I was okay and that my siblings were okay. Even though she went through hell, she did not walk away from her children!

Even with eight children, my mother loved me the same as my siblings. She treated us all the same. But, she couldn't control how our stepfather treated us. When I was locked in my bedroom, that was my stepfather's prerogative, not hers. My mother had no voice. She didn't have a voice where she could say, "Let Vicki out." She was fighting to stay alive daily.

I became furious at my mom because I did not understand why she stayed and why she didn't kill my stepfather in his sleep. As a child, I also didn't understand why I had to continue watching my mom get beaten, drugged, and set on fire. My second stepfather tried to set my mom on fire many times. I watched all of this happen.

If my mother were living and I had an opportunity to talk to her today, I would simply tell her that I love her. Despite and because of everything she went through that I didn't understand, I would say to her, "I love you for the fact that you loved us enough to stay. I love you for the fact that you loved us enough to put your life in danger—and it was in danger every single day. Yet, when you could walk away, you did not walk away. I love you for the fact that you taught me how to be strong."

Like my mother, I am a strong, resilient, religious mother to my children. My definition of motherhood is being the best mom you can be. As a mother, you are responsible for teaching, leading, guiding, and providing for your children. You are your kid's support system. You show them unconditional love in that you are the person they can turn to and depend upon no matter what.

The qualities I listed previously are essential to me for what it means to be a mother. Even though I've always wanted to be a mom, I only wanted two children: a boy and a girl. We had so many children in the family when I was a young girl. There was never enough of anything. I was tired of wearing hand-me-downs from the people down the street or the folks next door; I didn't want my children to have to go through that. I wanted my kids to have a good life. I wanted my children to have a trauma-free life. I didn't want them to go through any of what I went through as a child.

My children were good kids. They were just like any other kids. I raised them in a home where they had their mom and dad; even though I might have been more of a disciplinarian in the house, they still had the both of us. So they had a good upbringing. I am proud to say that my children went to school every day, and they never got into drugs or alcohol.

:::::

I played a different role in my children's lives than my mother did because I spent more quality time with my children. I could attend my son's basketball games, where I could scream and yell and call him the baby and embarrass him. With my daughter, I could attend to what she had going on in her school. I could go out and play on the playground or take a walk with them. When I was a child, my mom was not allowed to come off or step on the front porch. So she missed out on many things that she could have done with us when we were kids because my mom wasn't allowed to do those things.

My daughter believes that I showed favoritism toward my son when they were growing up, but that's not true. I think she looks at it that way because my daughter is more like me. She's a strong girl. My son seemed to be the child who needed more guidance. When he was going into school, I even kept him back one year because I felt he wasn't ready to let go of my shirttail. He was a mama's boy—and he just wasn't prepared to grow up yet.

As they got a little bit older, even as teenagers in high school or when they got out of school, my daughter went and found a job. She's like me; she'll work two or three jobs, no problem. My son thought his life was supposed to be a party. He didn't want a job that tied him down; he wanted a fun job. I didn't favor my son, but I adapted my parenting style when working with him because my son needed more guidance than my daughter.

In motherhood, I continued my mother's habit of singing while she cooked in the kitchen. I followed her example as far as attending church regularly; I love the church. But I considered what I wanted to take forward in my own family and what I wanted to leave behind. First, I wanted to ensure that no man ever abused me like my stepfather abused my mom. So my middle sister and I decided that we would never have any man who would hit us—and we have kept that promise.

As a mom, love your kids, take time out for them, teach them and guide them. Don't tell them to do or be something without first setting a good example with your own words and actions. Take care of your kids. Watch your children and the people that your kids are around. Also, watch the people you leave your children with when you need a babysitter. Don't put anybody over your children. Don't bring a man into your household, no matter how much you might love him until you truly know that person.

My mom passed on January 12, 1995, and this was the last letter she wrote.

Dear Lord, In the name of Jesus, I'm in an emotional state but crying sometimes helps to ease my pain. First, you know all about me, I'm your child, and I want to thank you for saving my soul and giving me the beautiful gift of the Holy Ghost. Lord, I need your help I have a problem that only you can solve, I know you are a just God, and I know you are my friend as well as my all and all, teach me the right words of prayer, give me understanding, help me to treat everybody right. Help me to be what you would have me to be in these last and evil days. I'm sincere as I know how to be, help me to crucify self—let your blood cover my entire body from head to toe. Your blood, the blood of Jesus.

I have a condition in my body I'm asking you to deliver me from kidney disease make them whole again and heal me from diabetes, and high blood pressure. I know you're able to bless my soul save me the more, running over with the holy ghost that's in me, have your way in my life, cover my husband with your blood, only you can help him, my son Noble, Rosetta, Vicki, Arlene, Curtis, Tyrone, Walter Jr., and their families. Give them the mind to give their life to you before it's too late, touch my mother's body cover her from head to toe with your blood, the blood of Jesus makes whole, bless our church and the saints everywhere Thank you, Jesus. You are so worthy to be praised, thanking you for what you have done and what

you are going to do, Thank You Jesus Glory to God. Praise Your
Holy Name, -ES

Last but not least, keep the faith—God has given me an unbelievable strength that I cannot explain to other people.

I can do all things through Christ that strengtheneth me — (Philippians 4:13)

ABOUT THE AUTHOR:

Social Media:

IG @gospelladyvh1

Email gospelladyvh@yahoo.com

Vicki Hill, also known as "The Gospel Lady," has been a radio gospel announcer at KISS 107.1 WTLZ for over twenty-six years. Thousands of people have invited Vicki into their homes every Sunday to listen to her words of encouragement and special music arrangements of contemporary Christian to traditional gospel music. In addition, the Gospel Lady has been the driving force in bringing 3,000 to 5,000 people to Gospel Fest held each year at Ojibway Island in Saginaw, Michigan. This event provides a safe place where all people of multi-cultural backgrounds and races can honor God collectively.

Vicki addresses groups at youth conferences and school mentors at the Saginaw County Juvenile Detention Center (monthly). She spearheads the annual Warm a Child for Winter project, which provides coats for underprivileged children. Vicki has also developed forums that deal with domestic violence, homosexuality, and suicide. When the community requests her presence, she travels to conferences, churches, and workshops and hosts countless events. Financially, Vicki also supports many organizations and churches' community initiatives. If she is available and the purpose is meaningful, "NO" is not an option.

Vicki has been the Branch Manager at the Jolt Credit Union in Bay City, Michigan, for twenty-six years and has enjoyed her career in the financial field for over thirty years. She is the Vice-Chair of

Women of Colors, where she was voted Woman of the Year in 2012 for her hard work, dedication, and commitment to the Great Lakes Bay Region.

ACKNOWLEDGMENTS

I want to thank God for His love and for giving me the inspiration and courage to write this book. I thank God for giving me a purpose, using me as His vessel, and guiding me toward my purpose. I pray this book inspires mothers and children to love unconditionally and to give hope no matter what you may be experiencing in life. A mother's love is one of God's trusted gifts.

I want to thank all the mothers who love their children unconditionally; I especially thank my mom, Dorothy Mae, for creating me. Her legacy lives on through her children. I am telling my mom's story because she could not tell her story. My mom showed me how to love unconditionally. I want to honor my mom in writing this book and encourage women to have faith and never give up on themselves and their children despite the difficulties.

Thank you to my sons, Jawain and Cawain, for allowing me to be your mother even when I made mistakes. Remember to live your life to the fullest and learn from your mistakes. Thank you to my husband, Patrick, for offering patience, letting me live my dreams, helping me raise my sons, and showing us new things in life we could have never imagined.

Thank you to my sister, Sandra, and friends Marcia, Lula, and Vicki for your courage and transparency in sharing your mothers' stories about motherhood, by which I know your mothers would be proud of the women you have become. I pray that you will not forget your mother's memories with this book.

Thank you to BOBM Publishing for contributing to the efforts in publishing this book and providing editorial assistance on the chapters featuring Sandra Kay Wooten, Marcia Reeves, Vicki Hill, Lula Woodard, and myself, Evelyn McGovern. I appreciate your creativity and hard work!

Thank you to Women of Colors (WOC) and the many women who have motivated me through the years to be stronger to lead this organization for over three decades successfully. Thank you to the entire Saginaw community for your continuous support.

ABOUT THE LEAD AUTHOR

Evelyn McGovern is the wife of Patrick McGovern. She is the mother of fraternal twin sons named Jawain and Cawain. Evelyn retired after 25 years of service with the City of Saginaw in Michigan. She also served in the Army Reserves for eight years and graduated from Delta College.

In 1993, Evelyn co-founded Women of Colors (WOC) and had served as the (acting) president since 1997. WOC is a grassroots nonprofit organization with a mission to promote diversity and enhance community relations in the Great Lakes Bay Region by empowering women and families, mentoring youth, performing community service, and collaborating with other organizations.

Other membership affiliations include HIV/AIDS Task Force; Family Youth Initiative Coalition; MSU–4H; Three Hundred Girls Committee; Healthy Community Partners Advisory Board; Saginaw Leadership Alumni/1000 Leaders Alumni; Saginaw Women in Leadership; Coalition That Cares; Behavior Health Action Group, Opioid Task Force; Saginaw County Prevention Coalition; Serves on the Board of Directors Saginaw Transit Authority Regional Services (STARS); and Community Police Advisory Commissioner (CPAC).

Evelyn has devoted countless hours to volunteerism and service to enrich the culture that makes the Saginaw community an excellent place for individuals and families to work, have fun, and live. She helped develop the City of Saginaw Special Events Committee and participated in the pilot City of Saginaw Labor-Management Leadership Team. It comprised frontline employees, management, police, and firefighters working together to make creative and constructive decisions to move the City in a positive direction; and developed the City of Saginaw's Green Team Committee and in-house recycling program. She also received the Saginaw County Chamber of Commerce Spirit of Saginaw Award in 2022. Evelyn believes in strengthening our community, and in doing so, people of all colors must work together, embrace diversity, and serve in any way possible.

Email:
motheryouknow@gmail.com
Facebook Page:
https://www.facebook.com/ewmcgovern
Instagram:
https://www.instagram.com/motheryouknow/
LinkedIn:
https://www.linkedin.com/in/evelyn-mcgovern-02a24521/